Persia Unveiled

The testimony of Jason DeMars, the Believers of Iran
and the Missions Work in Turkey

DEDICATION

To my wife, Amy, who stands with me through thick
and thin, a strong woman of faith and the love of my
life.

CONTENTS

PREFACE

Now that we are well into the 21st Century, it is sometimes difficult for some of us to understand certain concepts, such as the need for basic one-on-one missionary activity. With our instant communication capabilities we assume that if we know something here, then everyone on the planet must be equally knowledgeable. But as we know, that is simply not the case.

The original command from our Lord and Savior, as recorded in Mark chapter 16, is very simple and very far-reaching: "Go ye into all the world, and preach the gospel to every creature. He that believeth and is baptized shall be saved; but he that believeth not shall be damned."

Someone has to be called and anointed to go, others are called to help in the background, and it all works together very harmoniously, especially when there is a mutual respect and burden to fulfill the words of Jesus Christ. God never has judged or condemned without first sending a warning.

Jesus also said in John 6:37, "All that the Father giveth me shall come to me; and him that cometh to me I will in no wise cast out." Nothing at all can keep a predestined seed of God from reacting and blossoming upon contact with the Word and the Sprit of God. And only God knows the location of each seed and at what time and by what means He will bring that seed to life.

I know the author very well, Bro. Jason is a precious friend. He is doing his part to fulfill the Words of Jesus Christ.

In this book, Persia Unveiled, you will find heart-warming testimonies, their struggles and their victories, and yes, right here in our lifetime, not 400 years ago.

What you are reading here is simply the continuation of the Book of Acts of the Holy Spirit in the lives of believers in God's Word, right here, right now.

George Smith

Believers International

INTRODUCTION

I have had it in my heart for about five years to put together a book of how the Lord called me to Himself, led me to ministry to Iranian's and include within it testimonies of Iranian Muslim converts. It's been quite the journey to get here, but as I sit and assemble the various testimonies of this book and put together the research for historical details I feel a sense of fear. Not just that it is a big project, but that it will be presented in such a way that the glory of God will be seen and not me and what I am doing. I have one purpose in writing this book and that is that God will be glorified and that the truth will be shown forth. We are following the Scriptural message that God sent to us through William Branham and it has been spoken against and misunderstood by many. Since that message is true it should be attested to by the lives of those following it and the supernatural testimonies that come as a result. These are a few of these testimonies.

1 Peter 1:1 Peter, an apostle of Jesus Christ, to the strangers scattered throughout Pontus, Galatia, Cappadocia, Asia, and Bithynia,

Peter is writing to "strangers scattered throughout" and these words are very significant. The word "strangers" from the Greek means a "resident foreigner" and "scattered throughout" means the dispersed or dispersion. It is often spoken of as the "diaspora." In our world, today we often refer to them as "refugees." Peter is writing to refugees now living in "Pontus, Galatia, Cappadocia, Asia, and Bithynia." Each of these are regions within modern day Turkey. As Peter wrote and ministered to refugees in regions of ancient Turkey, we are now ministering to refugees in modern day Turkey, Alpha (the beginning of the church age) is becoming the Omega (ending of the church age). We're back to where we started from. God is moving in a might way among believers in the Middle East, especially the Farsi speakers. Those that speak Farsi or related dialects are Iranian's, Afghans and Tajik's. Iranians and Afghans are among those nationalities who are most turning to Christ. There is a great move of the Holy Spirit among them. We are grateful to be a small part of that.

CHAPTER 1

THE HISTORY OF THE GOSPEL TO IRAN AND MINISTRY BACKGROUND

Jeremiah 49:39
But it shall come to pass in the latter days that I will bring again the captivity of Elam, saith the Lord.

The Baker Encyclopedia of the Bible tells us that Elam is, "Occupying an area roughly the size of Denmark...located in southwest Asia, east of Babylonia and north of the Persian Gulf, on a plain known to the Iranians since the Middle Ages as Khuzistan." [1] The Elamites were once a people distinct from Medes and Persians, but have now been absorbed, along with the Medes, into what we now call "Iranians". Looking more closely at this Scripture there is no doubt it is referring to the captivity and restoration of a country. However, if we look at it spiritually, God is setting the people of Elam free--the Iranian people.

Today, there is a great move of Iranians leaving

---

[1] Baker Encyclopedia of the Bible

3

Islam and coming to Christianity--hundreds of thousands of them. The Christian Post reporting on figures from Elam Ministries, an Iranian ministry based in London, states, "The group said that 20 years ago, estimates put the number of believers in Iran at only 2,000–5,000 people, but new statistics are saying there could be anywhere between 300,000 to 1 million Christians in the country." [2] God is sweeping through the Persian-speaking peoples. They have become disgusted with the religion of Islam. They have seen the freedom which lies in Christianity and they are turning to it in large numbers. This move is unprecedented throughout the history of Islam. Mark Howard, writing for the Gospel Coalition writes, "As a result, more Iranians have become Christians in the last 20 years than in the previous 13 centuries put together since Islam came to Iran. In 1979, there were an estimated 500 Christians from a Muslim background in Iran. Today, there are hundreds of thousands—some say more than 1 million...In fact, last year the mission research organization Operation World named Iran as having the fastest-growing evangelical church in the world." [3]

[2] The Christian Post, article dated November 16, 2016, by Stoyan Zaimov,
http://www.christianpost.com/news/irans-house-church-movement-witnessing-astounding-growth-hundreds-being-baptized-171526/#xuKizGAqOWYFugTw.99

[3] Mark Howard, The Gospel Coalition, article dated July 30, 2016, https://www.thegospelcoalition.org/article/the-story-of-the-irans-church-in-two-sentences

The gospel net spoken of in Matthew 13:47 is being cast out in the Middle East and is creating a similar movement that occurred in the USA and Canada after World War II with many of the healing ministries when the net was cast out. Behind the revival that is sweeping the Persian-speaking people, there's been a message going forth, and that message is actually what is causing a separation between the good and bad fish. The fisherman go forth and cast the nets then they sit down and gather the good into vessels and cast the bad away. God draws the people and they respond. Although a minority, there are people that are responding to this Message and growing in this Message. We are thankful to be a part of that work.

As I testify of what God has done, I want to be clear that you don't think this is about me. When Brother Branham would share testimonies, he'd say, *it wasn't me. It wasn't me. You're not feeding on me. If it was up to me I would have a different life than I do today.* The choice to be a missionary was not mine, it was God's. I am thankful to be a witness and an instrument he can use to call out his people.

To lay the basic framework of the work we are doing with Iranian's I want to give this brief history. In the summer of 2009, Present Truth Ministries began sponsoring the translation work of brother Branham's messages into Farsi. The translations were from a family of brothers that started their ministry in Iran. Their mother is Congolese and their father is Iranian, and they came to the Message in Congo under the influence of

Ewald Frank, a German minister who knew brother Branham. They returned to Iran, and the Lord called them to a ministry. Many supernatural things happened in their ministry, and God directed them to begin a work of spreading the Message there. However, within 15 years, they only translated five sermons, most likely because they did not have a burden for translation.

As I began working with these brothers, my main emphasis was to encourage them toward more translation work. They found a brother named Mehdi Karbalaee Ali, which is the epitome of an Islamic name, so he changed his name to Nehemiah. I met him in Turkey in February 2011, on my first missions trip there; I found him to be a sincere, godly brother that took what the prophet said seriously and was very desirous to grow in the Message. Nehemiah became our main translator and has translated most of the messages that have been done. We have 51 translations as of the printing of this book, as well as 24 on audio. He has also become the main minister that we are working with in Turkey and he is also my main translator when I preach on many trips.

Nehemiah was eventually sentenced to six years in prison because of his faith, even while he was living in Turkey. We will get more details in further chapters. He decided to go through the UN refugee process and ended up being directed to Canada.

We are continuing to work on translating more Messages of brother Branham and this is a great burden we have for the spiritual growth of Iranian believers.

GOD CALLING

I grew up in a Christian home, we were Lutheran, but were Bible believers. My mother attended Bible Study Fellowship and I went with her and was in the children's classes. My mother taught me a tremendous reverence and respect for the Word of God. For much of my young life I played three sports; basketball, baseball and football. My family is a sports family, my father started the Youth Basketball Program in Columbia Heights, Minnesota and coached three sports over the years. My brother has been a Boys High School Basketball Head Coach for over 20 years. I was recruited to play basketball and football in college. That was my life.

I lived a clean, moral life, but was an overconfident, foul mouthed kid. At the end of my Senior Year in High School I got in with the wrong crowd and over time my will power was broken down and I began to drink and smoke marijuana. During this time, I needed to decide which college I would attend to play basketball and football. I remember sitting in my room in my parents' house and a voice spoke to me, "Go to Bethel College." This was a Baptist school, my other options were very good sports schools, but have long since abandoned their religious aspects. I called the football coach and the basketball coach to let them know. Then I went and told my parents. They were very shocked and happy, realizing I was in a rebellious state, but chose the

7

Christian school above the others.

I continued my rebellious activities at Bethel. Then the joy for sports began to leave me. I was treated unfairly by the coaches on the basketball team. Then my football coach wanted to move me from Quarterback to Wide Receiver. I had no desire to do that. So, suddenly I was done with athletics. I met two brothers who were on the track team, but enjoyed playing intramural basketball. We became good buddies. Their father was a conservative Presbyterian pastor in northern Minnesota. These two brothers began to discuss Calvinism and the doctrines of the Reformation with me. Frankly, I knew very little of what they were talking about. Even though I went through many Bible classes the main thing I learned growing up was "if the Bible says it, it's the truth." They would ask me, "do you believe in predestination?" I would say, "Well, I don't know. But you read a Bible verse with the word in it, so I believe what the Bible said."

They started to ask me, "well, if you believe it, then why do you live the way you do?" I just told them, "Look, I believe it and will one day live it, but now I'm just having fun." They told me that it doesn't work that way and told me about justification by faith and the new birth.

These conversations probably took place over a period of a year. Many of them took place at Buffalo Wild Wings and on the way home one Tuesday night I thought in my heart, "God, I want to live for you."

When I thought those words, I felt a weight lift from off my shoulders, felt clean in my heart and a new resolve to live for Christ. Something else happened within me and that is that my whole desire changed. Previously I had no desire to read anything but the sports page, but now I had a fervent desire to read and understand the word of God. I devoured the Scriptures and began reading the great works of the Reformation period and beyond. My favorites were Jonathan Edwards, John Calvin and Martin Luther. I remember one time sitting in the chair in my parents living room reading a large volume by Jonathan Edwards and my mom walked by and said, "who are you and what have you done with my son?" She was excited to see the change in me to say the least. She had prayed for it my whole life.

At that time, my college major was Business Marketing, but my desire was to change it to Theology to prepare myself for going to seminary. I had a strong call upon my life to Minister the Word. To have a major in Theology I would have had to continue my education at Bethel for another semester so my advisor suggested that I get a Major in Philosophy and take some Theology courses. This will allow me to go on to get my Masters of Divinity. I made the change in my major and went down the road to select which Seminary I would attend.

During this time, I was introduced to a friend of the two brothers who led me to the Lord. They said, "he's on fire for God, but has some strange doctrines, maybe we can straighten him out." We began to meet with him on a frequent basis and began to see just how much what he had to say made sense. He was an artist and he began illustrating a picture of a wheat plant. He explained how the Reformation started with Luther and other preaching justification by faith and this was the stalk that came forth out of the ground, then the tassel began to form and this was the Wesleyan movement of sanctification and then the shuck came, which looks very similar to the grain, and that was the Pentecostal restoration of the gifts and then after that it comes back to the original seed which is the restoration back to the original faith. He told me each of those Reformers had a message from the Lord, but they formed denominations from it. He began to introduce us to water baptism in the name of the Lord Jesus Christ and then gave me the Anointed Ones at the End Time tape, since I was a good Calvinist I absolutely loved the teaching on predestination and showing how the rain can fall on the just and the unjust and do the same signs and miracles, but it is the Word of God which differentiates the truth from the false. As I studied the message that William Branham was teaching it became more and more clear to me that it was the truth because the Bible became a new book to me and opened many things that I couldn't understand from Theology courses and the private studies I had done. I put it aside for a while, but then something led me to begin reading the Seven Church Ages book. As I read that I realized I needed to act and get rebaptized.

During the time that I expressed my interest in being rebaptized I started attending the message church in the area in addition to the Baptist church I attended. I really enjoyed it, but it came to a point I was concerned about myself and the direction I was going. I began to earnestly pray, remembering what I read that, we can never pray too much for revelation of the Scriptures. I got on my knees in my room with the door shut and the window was only open a very small crack and the shade was down. As I prayed and asked the Lord to show me the truth a wind came into the room and came across my back. I could even hear a swoosh sound as this wind came through the room. I turned and looked at the window and the shade was perfectly still. I saw this and then felt the Presence of a Great Being in my room that caused me to press my head into my bed in deep awe and reverence. I realize this was a supernatural event and the Holy Spirit was there in the room. When this happened to me there was such an assurance that this message is the truth. It isn't something that I can explain, but God placed within me that assurance.

It also reminded me of a time before I got saved. I was driving down the road with my two Presbyterian buddies and we stopped at a Stop sign late at night, around midnight. Both myself and one of the brothers looked up and then looked back at each other and then looked back up again. Above us there was an amber colored light hovering about fifteen feet above the car. Both of us immediately got the feeling of dread and fear within our hearts as we sat and stared at this light. This was the same feeling I had when in prayer in my room.

As time went forward I still was going on with my

idea that I needed to go to Seminary to be prepared for the ministry, but the more I listened to brother Branham and spoke with my pastor, brother Don Hoffman, the more I realized that what I needed was to step forward and begin to minister the Word according to my calling. In early 2000 while still at college I began to preach in my local church. As time went on I began to realize the Lord had called me for more than preaching in the local church. I had met several missionaries, the Lord had spoken to my heart not to limit my ministry to the four walls of this church and there was a burden there for more, but not knowing what to do or which direction to go.

When the translation work began in 2009, I was working for Wells Fargo as a loan processor. It was like having two full-time jobs as I was also working with the Iranians. I had such a burden for the mission work that it began to override my full-time job at Wells Fargo, and my work there began to suffer. The Lord had been calling me to leave my banking position and go full time into the ministry; but I could not see how that would work and told the Lord I could not do it. My grandfather worked at the same job for 55 years and my father worked at the same job for 35 years, and I've lived in two homes my whole life. Stability was both modeled and taught to me as I grew up. I continued to tell the Lord no for a whole year.

During this time, depression hovered over me. I faced many frustrations, difficulties and constant conviction over resisting His call. But God, knowing me as perfectly as He does, began to bring His loving kindness down upon me in the form of a hammer, as it were.

In the spring of 2012, God spoke to me through three brothers who had no idea what I was going through or what the Lord was speaking to me. No one knew the extent of my struggle other than my wife. The Lord spoke first during a testimony meeting in a Somali neighborhood. One of the Iranian brothers in our church stood up and began to testify,

When God sends us on a mission, sometimes we have trouble with that. But when our boss at our work says, "I am going to have you go to another city," we understand immediately that he is going to provide for our transportation, our food, gas, whatever we have need of to get our job completed. We have such confidence in this that we do not even question it. But then when God calls us, we doubt and wonder how it will happen.

Tears began streaming down my face and I said, Okay, Lord. I know what you're telling me, but it's going to be hard. He spoke again to me during a church service the next Wednesday evening. At one point, the brother ministering said, You're thinking in your mind, [and I was] when God calls you to do something, you're thinking, 'But what about my family? How am I going to provide for them? How can I take care of them?' You don't think God can take care of your family? I began thinking, But what about my retirement and my future? The brother continued, "You don't think God has your future all in mind and that He won't provide for it?"

I decided to prostrate myself before the Lord. I prayed, I know that I must surrender to your will, but this is really hard. I'm not sure how or when or what you have in store for me. This scares me. But I want to follow You.

The next day, a brother in the church emailed a group quote. In the quote, Brother Branham was talking about Joshua:

Now, Joshua, in all this, knowing that the command was great; but, having the assurance, he could be fearless. He could be, as we'd call it, reckless, as long as he was pointed the right way. He might break up against a hill that would knock him backwards, but he was carried the right way. 56 So can the Church of the living God be reckless and fearless, in faith, if we're pointed the right way. For, He said, "As I was with Moses, I'll be with you. I'll not fail you nor forsake you." He never forsaken Moses. He never failed Moses. He will not fail Joshua. He will not fail us. He'll be with us. [4]

I was reading this on my cell phone in my car, and as I read through to the end, I took my phone and dropped it into the passenger seat. I said, *Lord, it is so obvious what you are calling me to do. But I do not know when this is to be or how. This is hard for me.* But I also knew that if it was God calling me, I could not run away from it, as hard as I may try; as much as I ran, I could not run away from the purpose he planned to accomplish through me.

---

[4] 60-0911M - As I Was With Moses, So I Will Be With Thee, Rev. William Marrion Branham, http://table.branham.org

It still took me four more months to figure out what to do and how to do it.

My wife had more peace about it than I did. She said, *I know you are going to leave your job, and I know that God has called you to do this.* We went to our family cabin to spend some time talking and praying over it. I finally said, *Well, I am going to tell my boss that in one month I will be leaving my job.*

I went to my boss and told him I was putting in my one-month notice. I told him I would be going into the ministry full time and he replied, *Well, you don't have to give a one-month notice, you can give two weeks.* And that was that.

It's been since August 2012, I still have worries and concerns, battling against the enemy to remain strong in faith. I often wonder how we are going to make it each month. Yet God has been faithfully providing and meeting our needs month by month. How he does it, I do not know. But because it was his calling, he provides. My humanness still loves its comforts, but I love the Lord with all my heart and will surrender to him and what he asks of me with everything that is within me.

CHAPTER 2

THE BEGINNING

In 2008, before the translating began, I was in a backslidden state of sorts. I was preaching, but my heart was not on fire for God. I was still in the ministry, but I knew I was not where I was supposed to be. When I was working full time, I had been learning internet marketing for building a network marketing business. Much of my time, effort and focus had gone into that.

My pastor began preaching in church about how we are using our time. How much are we dedicating ourselves to God? I began to come under conviction. At one point, the Lord spoke and said, *I want you to use what you have learned about internet marketing for my kingdom. I* didn't know exactly how to do that or what to do, but I knew that I loved this Message and its teachings. I began to write and record videos. I put them on YouTube, Myspace, and Facebook and began to build a subscriber base. I did Google AdWords as well, and received a lot of traffic to the Present Truth Ministries site. We also got in touch with people in Africa and India and received many invitations. However, I always had it in mind that

I was going to work with someone that was alone: someone who did not have help from anyone else.

One day I got an email from a man in Istanbul. He said, *I'm an Iranian, and we have churches and Message believers in churches in Iran, and we have one here in Turkey. I'd like you to come and visit us here in Turkey.* When I got that email, I thought, *Well, I'd be glad to help him, but I'm sure not going to Turkey. That sounds dangerous.* We stayed in touch and learned of some of their needs. We found out how few Message books they had translated, and it became such a burden for me to begin translation work. And so, we began.

Initially, my focus had been to get the Message into the hands of the people in Turkey and Iran, and to help them have the proper understanding and balance in the Message. However, in the Autumn of October 2009, there was a wave of arrests of ministers in the churches in Iran, including a minister named Youcef Nadarkhani who was facing the death sentence, for apostasy from Islam. The brother in Istanbul contacted me and asked if I would please advocate for these ministers. I told him I was just beginning internet marketing and that I did not have many contacts. However, I said I would be willing to write some articles and post them online to spread the word.

Thus, I began writing articles and getting in touch with different ministers and people around the Message. It also had begun to take up a very large amount of my time as I was still working my banking job during this period. During every break, and a few unscheduled breaks, I would walk up and down the hallway talking to contacts about the persecution cases and communicating with the brothers in Iran and in Turkey over what was going on. I continually worked on the persecution cases.

At the time, I had no contacts at all with any sort of persecution agencies or with the State Department. Everything I did was from scratch, but God began to open doors. I believe it was Voice of God Recording's that began putting updates on their website about the persecution. A brother in Arizona named Tim Amalong was flying out of the same airport that Congresswoman Gabrielle Giffords was also flying out of. They were able to have a conversation, and Tim mentioned to her that there was a man in Iran that was under the death sentence for apostasy and that the media was completely silent about. Nobody seemed to know about it.

Congresswoman Giffords replied that she was on the Human Rights Committee in the House of Representatives and had a contact within the State Department. She continued, they would be having a meeting about it in the next couple of days and would forward it on to the State Department.

And so, it was that just a couple of days later I received a call from the State Department. They asked me some questions as well as for some information. They carefully and critically examined the information with some of their allies that they had on the ground in Iran and were able to confirm it. From that time forward, they began working behind the scenes to help free Nadarkhani.

The ACLJ, American Center for Law and Justice, also got involved and began working with us and advocating for us. When Brother Nadarkhani was going through trial, the attorney and Chief Counsel for the ACLJ, Jay Sekulow, was constantly in contact with me asking what the latest news was since he appeared on many news stations including Fox News, CNN, and CBN. We, ourselves, were getting the news from a pastor within Iran who was right outside the courtroom and he would pass on the information within moments of hearing it, himself. The news was getting out so fast that the judge in the Iranian courtroom said, *Which one of you are informing these international news agencies?*

Shortly thereafter, the State Department called me and said the President would be issuing a statement about Nadarkhani's imprisonment and they would like me to read the statement before it went out to make sure everything was accurate. The Press Secretary then said they would issue the statement so that people, worldwide would have this information.

The Lord can open doors when he wants to open doors. All we can do is walk forward by faith. We realize who we are in Christ without exalting ourselves, yet we know that he has a great purpose for each of us. When he calls us to do something, he will open the door, and we can walk forward in faith and with confidence in his calling. We will still have struggles, concerns, worries or fears, but we must continue to persevere, moving forward.

Brother Nehemiah

Brother Nehemiah, as I mentioned before, is a gifted translator. He has never attended a university, but God gifted him and prepared him throughout his life for a translation ministry. To translate properly it requires more than just the mechanics of translating. There is a revelation behind the Message that brings a passion and reality to life. If a person does not have the revelation, all their translating will be in vain. We have been blessed that God has given Nehemiah this gift to translate along with the revelation of his Word.

Brother Nehemiah was born and raised in a very serious Muslim family. His birth name was Mehdi Karbalaee Ali, but this being an Islamic name, he changed it to Nehemiah Ardavan. His mother was the third wife (think polygamy) of his father. She was 12 years old and he was 45 years old when they were married. His father had a space dedicated to Muslim services where they worshipped their god. One month each year for 10 days they participated in a holiday called the *Day of Ashura* where they mourned the death of Imam Hussein, the grandson of Mohammad, and they beat and cut themselves. Brother Nehemiah was raised in this atmosphere, practicing Shia Islam and following the Quran. He was honored to be a Muslim and every night before bed he would say, "I testify La ilaha illa Allah, Muhammad rasoolu Allah." These were the necessary phrases to become a Muslim and he would say them to make sure that if he died, he would die a Muslim and go to heaven. In Arabic, it means, "There is no true god (deity) but Allah, and Muhammad is the Messenger of God."

As a result, he joined a part of the militia in Iran called Basij. According to the BBC:

"The Basij militia is an Iranian volunteer force of Islamic government loyalists which is often called out onto the streets at times of crisis to dispel dissent. The force was originally set up by Ayatollah Khomeini in 1979 as a resistance force during the Iran-Iraq war. They received limited training and were used for "human wave" attacks, for example being asked to clear Iraqi minefields by walking across them." [5]

Because of how the governmental leadership structure is set up, had he continued in the Basij, he could have been a VEVAK [6] agent (like our FBI and

---

[5] BBC News, Profile: Basij militia,
http://news.bbc.co.uk/2/hi/middle_east/8106699.stm

[6] The Ministry of Intelligence of the Islamic Republic of Iran وزارت اطلاعات جمهوری اسلامی ایران :Persian) Vezarat-e Ettela'at Jomhuri-ye Eslami-ye Iran) is the primary intelligence agency of the Islamic Republic of Iran and a member of the Iran Intelligence Community. It is also known as VAJA and previously as VEVAK (Vezarat-e Ettela'at va Amniyat-e Keshvar) or alternatively MOIS. It was initially known as SAVAMA, when it took over the previous regime's intelligence apparatus. The ministry is one of the three "sovereign" ministerial bodies of Iran due to nature of its work at home and abroad. Wikipedia,
https://en.wikipedia.org/wiki/Ministry_of_Intelligence

CIA) or joined the Iranian Revolutionary Guard and fought for Islam in Israel. For as many years as he spent connected to the military, he could never see any sign of God or any results of prayer. In fact, the more he prayed, the less he received. All he saw among the Revolutionary Guards, the Basij, and other religious parties was hypocrisy. He witnessed women raped, members stealing, drug abuse and dealing, fornication, and many other forms of wickedness. All of this brought him to the conclusion that there was no God. Of all the places, he thought he should be able to see God, it should be there where they were worshipping in all sincerity. He would wake up in the middle of the night to say the regular prayers and then continue praying and reading the Quran for an hour or two. But there was always something missing and no results or response from God. Finally, he said, "You know, there is no God...let's enjoy our life and enjoy everything we do. We'll get the results in this world."

For about eight years he did not believe in anything and proceeded to do many wicked things during that time. Because of how he acted and cursed, people did not want to be around him. He became friendless and alone. With no one to talk to he said to himself, "Maybe there is one God and I should find him because I lost everything. I wanted to make life better, but I only made it worse. So, let me find God."

He went back to the Quran and began to read it again, and again he found nothing. He began to read the holy book Avesta and many other books and teachings on the Iranian national religion called Zoroastrianism. He loved the history of it all but did not find God there either. While at work, he would do crossword puzzles and one clue was "One of the Gospels." Each time the answer was "Gospel of Mark." In Farsi, they call it *Marqos* but he could not even pronounce it and called it *Marqas.* He had no idea what that was and wondered if it was a food or some kind of cake…he just did not know.

One day he called his mom who was out shopping and said, "Would you please get me a Gospel of *Marqas*?"

She said, "What are you talking about? What is this?"

"It is just a book. Go to the bookstore and get me one," he responded.

She agreed to try to find one but was not able to find any available. However, she said their neighbor would get one for him. Their neighbor was like a female imam and was extremely religious and serious about her faith. So, her willingness surprised brother Nehemiah and he was not certain she would get him the book.

However, the next day she brought him a New Testament as well as a booklet called *"Footsteps of God in the Plan of Salvation."* He read the booklet and thought it was fantastic, but when he read the New Testament and the first few chapters of the Gospel of Mark, he thought it was complete nonsense and did not like it. He didn't think it was possible for a prophet to call a race of people a dog.

Brother Nehemiah continued on with his life until a couple months later when his mom came and told him,

"You know son, I read that book and I read that little booklet and I met with Jesus in my dreams and He said, "I am the Way, the Truth and the Life". I know that He is the Lord and Savior and I believe in Him."

Brother Nehemiah responded, "Come on, what are you talking about, Mom? What if I brought you a Buddhist book...would you turn Buddhist and say Buddha is God? What if I brought you the Torah? Would you say that Moses is God?"

"No, the only thing I know is that I met with Jesus. Jesus in person told me that He is a Savior and I believe in Him. I will just pray for you," his mom answered.

A couple weeks later, brother Nehemiah's sister came and told him she now believed in Jesus as her Lord and Savior also and that she as well had a dream where Jesus appeared to her and said, "I am the Way and the Truth and the Life".

"Come on!" he exclaimed, "What corruption I have brought to my family with my own hands." He called up his religious neighbor who asked if he had any questions. He told her he had thousands of questions even though he really wanted to report the pastor to the authorities. He was told there was a man who could answer his questions and a meeting was set up with him.

Brother Nehemiah went to the meeting full of pride in himself and his knowledge. He was ready to verbally outmaneuver the man, make the man realize he did not know anything, and then proceed to call the police to have the man arrested for ruining his family. However, when he arrived and began listening to the man, he was amazed. Everything the man was telling him was reasonable with everything in its place. It was wonderful and brother Nehemiah knew it was right and was close to converting to Christianity, but instead he ran. He could not yet accept it because deep in his heart he still considered himself a Muslim. He told the man, "You know what? Whatever you told me, I will find it in the Quran even better than that because the Quran is the most perfect book in the world."

He began reading the Quran again. He read it in Farsi, Arabic and in every other translation that was available. Yet he received nothing. The man called him to ask if he would like to meet again and brother Nehemiah agreed. Again, as brother Nehemiah listened to the man, he came very close to converting and again he ran. The man told him, "All religions and all beliefs have someone who will be very good at convincing you that they are right. Do not trust anyone, including me. But there is Somebody that cannot lie. This is not His characteristic and this is God Himself; and I can prove to you that He knows Farsi as well. He is the author of everything. Go and talk to Him in Farsi."

Brother Nehemiah decided he had nothing to lose and agreed to do it. For two weeks, he heard nothing but silence and was becoming disappointed. And then one day as he was praying in his room, he heard a very strong Voice in Farsi that brought him to his knees in fear. The Voice said, "I am the Way, the Truth, and the Life."

Brother Nehemiah knew he was not high on drugs because it was the middle of the day. Thoughts ran through his head, "What was that? Just ignore it, you know sometimes you talk. Maybe your mind was busy with something. Just ignore it. It was nothing."

Four weeks later he heard the very same Voice again say, "I am the Way, the Truth and the Life." He could not understand it or figure out what is was so he called the man right away even though it was 2 am. The man told him to come over the next afternoon.

However, the man did not explain anything to brother Nehemiah. Instead he just encouraged him to pray continually. Brother Nehemiah was disappointed. He had gone for answers and received none. But he went home and continued to pray.

The third time the Voice said, "It is hard for you to kick against the goads."

He just could not understand what was going on so he called the man again and said, "I need an answer. Would you please show me the answer right now?"

The man said to come over and he would show him the answer. When brother Nehemiah arrived, the man opened his little Bible, turned to St. John and showed him where the Lord Jesus says, "I am the Way, the Truth and the Life." Then he turned to the Book of Acts and showed him where Jesus met Paul on the road to Damascus and said, "It is hard for you to kick against the goads."

Something finally broke inside of brother Nehemiah

and he began weeping. He repented and received Christ into his life.

Following his conversion, he still did many worldly things. But God, in His infinite grace, put him in a process to bring him back to Himself and he is so thankful to the Lord for that.

In 2010, brother Nehemiah was preaching in a house church of 5 or 6 Christians when 25 VEVAK agents with Tasers and pistols burst in. They had all kinds of questions and paperwork, and then arrested brother Nehemiah on the spot and took him to Evin prison. According to the Muslim religion, a Muslim that converts to another religion is considered an apostate and deserves to die.

He was in prison for 33 days and for 19 of them he was in solitary confinement. The first 19 days, the agents led him to believe that his whole family had been arrested. While he was in the interrogation room, he could hear his mom in one room, one sister in another, and one sister in even another room all being interrogated. However, in truth his family was not in those rooms. They had instead been asked to the courtyard for questioning and interrogation where their voices were recorded. Then the agents played these recordings in 3 different rooms around brother Nehemiah so that he thought they were all imprisoned. He believed they were all being interrogated and tortured. This is considered a soft or mental torturing - a psychological torture.

They were also putting pressure on brother Nehemiah to recant his faith. If he did, he could walk out. But he kept refusing. As a result, during an interrogation they brought him a paper and asked him to sign it. He signed it and asked, "What was that?"

"It is not a big deal," they said. "It was your execution paper." Then they blindfolded him and walked him down a hall to a certain place. They put a rope around his neck and grabbed it and said, "Okay, moment of truth. You are going to recant or you are going to die."

Brother Nehemiah was very scared and prayed, "What should I do, God?" A few months earlier, a minister had testified of a similar situation and now God brought the minister's answer to his accusers back to Nehemiah's mind. He said, "You are asking me to recant my faith to save my soul; to save my life. What if I walk out of here and die in a car crash? I would have recanted my faith to save my life just to lose it. And what if I meet Jesus and He shows me His hands. What would I say? So, this is a terrible and hard thing and I'm very scared, but I would rather die here than to die like that. So, do whatever you want to do."

After that, the good cop/ bad cop games began. They said, "You know what? We didn't take him to court - the judge has not confirmed the verdict yet. We can do this whenever we want." They took him back to his cell where he shook for a couple of hours before he could mentally and physically calm down from that experience.

Meanwhile, while he was in prison, his mom had been coming to beg for information about him because no one told her where they were holding him. Every day for 33 days, from 8 in the morning to 8 at night, she was at the prison asking for information about her son. Many other mothers were there as well doing the same thing.

Some are mothers of political activists waiting for their family members and they have no clue as to where they are. After a while, some of them receive only a dead body. Nehemiah's mother told him that as she came to the prison one day, she heard a mother weeping. She asked what had happened and others around her responded, "Yesterday this lady was here and asked to visit her son. They said, 'Tomorrow you can come back and get your son. He is going to be released.' Today she was so happy. She came to get her son but they delivered her the dead body." Nehemiah's mom was so afraid that this would happen to her as well.

During Nehemiah's stay in solitary confinement, he never saw light, he was never let out, there was no fresh air, and he just sat in the cell while being interrogated. But while he was in prison, he learned for himself that Jesus Christ is the same yesterday, today and forever. His faith grew stronger, contrary to what they were trying to accomplish, and he had wonderful fellowship with the Lord. He spent much time fasting and praying, God spoke to, encouraged, and strengthened him.

His testimony today is that the Lord is alive - not

dead. He is a living God and whatever He did in the beginning, His Word is and remains the same and He can change your life. When he thinks about his life, his mind goes back to his favorite hymn, "Amazing grace how sweet the sound that saved a wretch like me..." What he was, how he was living and how God utterly changed his life and turned him into a completely new person is truly God's amazing grace over His child.

CHAPTER 3

BROTHER BEHNAM IRANI

Brother Behnam Irani is originally from Rasht, Iran, he had a ministry throughout Iran and was served six years in prison for his faith. He now lives in Turkey with his family.

He was born into a Muslim family and as a result he was immersed in Islam. When a baby is born in Iran, they say the prayer call into its ears. This type of upbringing meant being exposed to the propaganda and doctrine of Islam, as well as continually practicing Muslim rituals as the child grow.

Whether Behnam was at home, school or in the workplace, he was constantly immersed and exposed to Islam in many ways. To be a good Muslim it was required to learn the Koran, sing it, and learn and say the required prayers five times each day, have times of fasting, and attend the different holidays of Islam, especially the events during Ashura [7] and Tasua [8] in the

---

[7] For Shi'a Muslims, Ashura marks the climax of the Remembrance of Muharram,[8] and commemorates the death of Husayn ibn Ali, the grandson of Muhammad at the Battle of Karbala on 10 Muharram in the year 61 AH (in AHt:

month of Muharram. The constant immersion of these practices built faith and trust in one's subconscious, and they would think how fortunate and privileged they were to be born into this religion - that it was God's mercy upon them. This mind set prevented one from having any other ideas and would slowly possess the Muslim. Behnam really liked Islam as a teenager, and he participated in Koran competitions as well as group prayers in school.

At one point, Behnam had such a hunger to have an experience with God. In Islam, there is a prayer called the *Night Time Prayer* that is said to do just that, but one must wake up at midnight to say it. Brother Behnam was so desirous for an experience that he would wake up at 1:30 or 2 am to say those prayers and to ask God to visit him. Knowing that he was saying those prayers, people around him would say, "Behnam, how bright is your face! How spiritual you seem!" And yet within himself, he was struggling. He began to face the reality that what people said they saw in him was not actually what was going on inside. No matter how hard he tried, the lack of inner satisfaction continued to bother him.

October 10, 680 CE). The massacre of Husayn with a small group of his companions and family members had a great impact on the religious conscience of Muslims, particularly Shi'a Muslims, who commemorate Husayn's death with sorrow and passion.[9] Mourning for Husayn and his companions by his surviving relatives and supporters began almost immediately after the Battle of Karbala. -Wikipedia, https://en.wikipedia.org/wiki/Ashura

[8] The day before Ashura

Meanwhile, Behnam's older brother, Bahram, came to Christ in the Assemblies of God church in Rasht, Iran. The same time that he accepted Christ, Behnam began to hang out with the wrong crowd. The lack of answers during his prayer times made him look elsewhere for satisfaction. He began attending parties, smoking cigarettes, and participating in all kinds of worldly things that only resulted in polluting his soul.

He was seventeen years old when he was first arrested and imprisoned for his mischievous behavior. However, his imprisonment only gained him more respect among his friends as proof that he was a "good criminal," and somehow this graduated him to another level within his circle of friends. He liked how that felt.

During this time, Bahram kept sharing the gospel with him and asking him to leave the lifestyle he was leading and make a better life for himself. But the more his brother talked, the less Behnam heard. Behnam and his family members conspired to mock Bahram's faith and prevent him from any kind of religious activities. However, Behnam's time for military service arrived, and he was sent to Bandar Abbas, in Southern Iran, where narcotics, alcohol, and everything imaginable was available to him.

His brother did not give up on him however and kept mailing Behnam evangelical tracts. Out of respect for his brother, he would read them, but he had no intention of listening to what they had to say. After two years, he finished his military service, and he returned home. Six months later he was in a car crash that injured his leg, thigh and hip and resulted in 6 years of rehabilitation.

Though he did not realize it at the time, the accident became a blessing to him. God had been trying to speak to him through his brother, but he had not been listening. So, God used the accident to stop him and ask, "Where are you going?" And Behnam realized that he was quickly headed towards hell. While he recovered, he began to read the New Testament, and the scripture in Mark that talks about it being better to enter eternal life with one hand than to go to hell with two hands became very meaningful to him.

Brothers and Sisters from the Assemblies of God church would visit Behnam and sing songs, talk with him, and pray for him. This was a strange time for him, being neither Muslim nor Christian, and he felt under such pressure that he kept asking God to show him a way out. He would pray and cry every night for God to show him if Christ was real. And within two weeks, God visited him 4 times.

Behnam will never forget the last dream he had from the Lord:

"I saw Christ in the corner of my dream and He had stretched His arms, waiting for me. I heard a voice like a thunder from heaven telling me, 'Yes! Yes! This is the way you ought to go.' The voice stayed still...I could hear him in my ears."

It was 5 am when he awoke from the dream. He immediately went and woke his brother up saying,

"Wake up! I'm going to repent. I have to do it right now." And Behnam gave his heart to Christ.

The following Sunday he went to church and made a public confession of his faith, and that was when his new life began at age 24. In less than 3 months, he saw a phenomenal change in his life. All his desires, ways of thinking, and the standards in which he evaluated life changed. He could now see himself as a son of God. Over the next four years he stayed in the Assemblies of God church and witnessed to many people, bringing many people into the church.

[On a side note, during that time in Iran, coming to Christ was like a nuclear blast. There were many serious consequences. Family and friends would consider the convert an apostate, therefore, unclean, and many were disowned by their families and removed from their parent's will. And yet, when one had a personal experience with the Lord, they were not able to deny or reject it, no matter the cost. These days, Iranians are more familiar with the concept of coming to Christ due to Christian broadcast on the many satellite channels available and outreach from churches. And yet, these steps have come because of the many persecutions, shedding of blood, and imprisonment of believers.]

One morning while brother Behnam was praying, he heard a voice from the Lord say, *"Get out of Babylon and like a goat, go in front of the flock"* [Jeremiah 50:8]. He did not understand this and, in fact, it made him nervous. He went to a deacon at his church and told him what he had heard. He asked the deacon what the scripture meant and what God was trying to tell him. The deacon said, "Brother Behnam, this is a dangerous scripture because it is asking you to get out of Babylon. And you being in charge means that the church is Babylon."

Brother Behnam had no reference of what the message was until a few months later when he went to Armenia to meet two brothers from Switzerland and Italy that were ministering the message there. While preaching, one of the ministers began talking about leaving Babylon. This struck brother Behnam's heart, and following the service he talked more with the brothers about the message of the hour. They were able to explain the message and give him a greater perspective and understanding of what it was all about. After hearing the truth, he decided to leave the Assemblies of God church, which caused a whole new set of difficulties.

Around this time, many people were being persecuted and killed by the government of Iran, and as a result, many Iranian believers were leaving the country. It was similar in many ways to the dark ages. So not only was Behnam under pressure from the government of Iran, but now he was receiving it from the denominational churches as well. During all of this, he had a new message to preach and a new ministry to begin. He and some other brothers were the first group to start house churches and to organize prayer meetings. They began with 7 or 8 single brothers and sisters and continued to share the Gospel. They would hold 4 to 5 hour services straight without being tired. They were energetic, full of dreams, inspired and desired to do something for the kingdom of God.

It was not long before a few families came to Christ and joined the group, and the single brothers and sisters also married and found their own places to live. The home church was increasing in number with more houses and more families. The work of God increased in Rasht to the point where Behnam and another brother named Khandjani felt led by God to lay hands on yet another brother named Youcef to ordain him as a pastor in Rasht. Behnam and Khandjani then moved to Tehran and rented a place for Khandjani's family as they began sharing the gospel there in Tehran. And again, they established a church and began worshipping the Lord there.

Shortly after, Behnam got married and their numbers continued to increase to the point where it was necessary to have different services during the week. Either Behnam would host them, Khandjani or his parents.

Meanwhile, they were called to report to VEVAK's office where they were interrogated and asked to stop their operations. The officials began to ask other church members to report in for questioning as well. This continued until Behnam felt it was time to leave the church in Tehran to Khandjani and move on to another province. Their goal was to keep moving forward and to spread the message of the hour to all the different provinces and cities in Iran.

God led Behnam to the city of Karaj where he began his ministry. Many people came to Christ and the work kept increasing. Children, teenagers, young people and families were all coming in and as a result, they needed more ministers and more services.

Early one winter morning, Behnam awoke early to attend his grandparent's funeral when he heard a knock at the door. It was only 7 am, but the person said he had a package for him from the post office. As soon as he opened the door, five people walked in. One man began videotaping everything while the others began going through his personal belongings, the church chairs, and everything else they could fine. They also wanted to take the church sound system. Their goal was to put pressure on him and frighten him.

This being a nationwide operation, they arrested Behnam as well as his brother Bahman and took them to Karaj prison in section 8, which is known to be the toughest facility. They were each put in solitary confinement and were interrogated for ten days straight. Sometimes they were insulting, sometimes they were violent, and on one occasion, 3 of the agents interrogated him at the same time. It took 14 hours to go through all their questions, and they continually pressured them to sign a paper promising to stop any evangelical operation and to shut down all the churches.

One night around midnight, they came to Behnam's cell, blindfolded him, and brought him to a room. They removed the blindfold, and he found himself in a small courtroom-like setting with the general attorney's representative and another representative present. He was told that they had his execution verdict confirmed and he would be hanged.

By God's grace, he had such a peace within him. He looked at the representatives and told them that there is a scripture in the Bible that says, "For me, to live is Christ and to die is gain."

"What does that mean?" One of the men asked.

Behnam explained, "If I live, I'm living for the glory of God, and if I die, so be it because I will be in glory."

"Aren't you afraid?"

Behnam replied, "By God's grace, no."

After that, everything changed. He was told he could be released on bail, and within 24 hours he was out of prison. It was his first imprisonment, and even though other brothers in other cities were also arrested, Behnam received the one of longest sentences of a 5 years suspended sentence. This normally meant he just had to be more cautious and careful, but a few months later, he was summoned to court again. The agents were holding one of the booklets that Behnam had written. In the booklet, Behnam went through King David's sins and how his sins were forgiven him. He mentioned that there was no sinless man. In Islam, 2 of the Imams are sinless saints. The agents used this booklet to falsely accuse Behnam of insulting the doctrines of Islam and Islam itself. They immediately transferred him to prison where he stayed for 3 days before being released.

Despite all of this, brother Behnam and the other brothers kept on with their ministry. The churches were increasing and the message was sent to many surrounding cities. They worked with denominations and shared booklets and materials with believers amongst the churches. They were very well known in Iran by this time which prompted the government to execute another attack on the church. While agents invaded the homes, and arrested some brothers, Behnam was to meet with other ministers in Karaj when he realized there was a van and other cars parked in front of where they were to meet. Realizing they were there to arrest them, he immediately called the other ministers and told them not to come. He felt the agents were waiting until they were all together so they could arrest them all at once. Miraculously, Behnam was able to escape.

He went to Armenia and stayed for three months. However, things were not going well back in Iran, and he felt led to return. Secretly and discreetly he returned and began holding meetings again. During a service several months later, fully armed agents came in and began beating him. They handcuffed him behind his back and threw him to the ground on his face. From the meeting, they took him back to his home, grabbed a few things, and took him to prison. Behnam's family was not home but in Tehran during his arrest.

For two months, no one was given any information

on his whereabouts. These were very difficult days. There were constant interrogations, mental and psychological pressures, all kinds of threats concerning his wife, and many other things to make a person nervous and scared. For 75 days, he was held in solitary confinement until he was finally released once again on bail.

Shortly after his release, they sentenced him to one year in prison which they appealed, and it was reduced to eight months. In the spring of 2010, brother Behnam was transferred to prison where he served his eight months. The day before he was to be released, he was informed that he would have to serve the 5-year suspended sentence from his earlier verdict. This was extremely difficult news on many levels, but what concerned him the most at that moment was his two-year-old son, seven-year-old daughter, and the fact that he was not allowed to call his wife, Kristina, to let her know what was going on. He was so worried for them and the pressures and difficulties he knew they would have to face.

Prison conditions in Iran are very poor and unsafe and are managed independently as private sectors. Weapons are made within the prison, and narcotics among other things are smuggled in as well. It is easy but very expensive to access them once they are in. Raping inmates is also a common thing that they are not willing to put a stop to.

Political and religious prisoners are supposed to have a cell block to themselves, but instead, they are held with all other prisoners. This doubles the pressure for the political and religious prisoner. Also, the prisons are populated significantly beyond their capacity. In cell number 7 where Behnam was held, the standard population should be around 200 prisoners; instead there was 600-700 of them in the same cell block. That meant that about 200 of them basically lived in the prison yard no matter the weather and came in only at night to sleep in the hallway on the floor. There is absolutely no privacy and personal health is a disgrace.

This overpopulation also caused constant fighting over one's personal health and food. Inmates are required to buy their own food from the prison stores which supply only very low quality brands and lack any sort of basic nutrition. Prisoners are managed in the prison with their own finances. If one would like to upgrade their food, repair or replace toiletries, or receive medical attention for example, the inmate must pay for it themselves. This makes prison even harder on the poor people since they have no money to spend.

When a prisoner does require medical attention, there is no access to medicine, and the doctors treat them with disrespect. With conditions as they are, there are also many contagious diseases. On the previous occasion when Behnam was held in prison for 75 days, he came out with bone problems. After a year in central prison, he developed an intestinal bleeding problem but received no medical attention. By God's grace, constant follow ups, and outside pressures, the prison received a court order requiring them to transfer him to a hospital under heavy security. However, Behnam was given a paper to sign agreeing to pay for the surgery himself, and they denied his request for a medical time out to take care of his health before being transferred back to prison. They proceeded to handcuff his hands to the bed and then chained his legs to the bed. They admitted him to a low quality public hospital in Karaj where they could not solve the problem and performed an unsuccessful surgery. He was transferred back to prison within 24 hours with no time for recovery.

Behnam was also not allowed access to a Bible in prison. However, sixteen months after he was arrested, he managed to smuggle a Bible in through another inmate, as well as smuggle in ten booklets of brother Branham for his own personal reading through one of the prison guards he had befriended by this time. Unfortunately, a few months later his cell was searched and his Bible was confiscated. Although he wrote many letters to the prison authorities asking for the return of his Bible, he never saw it again.

And yet, during all of this, Behnam desired to share the gospel and be a witness in the hand of the Lord to his fellow inmates. This can be difficult in prison because most of the prisoners are drug addicts and unstable; but the Lord went before him, and he was able to establish a Narcotics Anonymous meeting inside the prison within a few months. Eventually, with much opposition but also the support of several other inmates, this turned into obtaining four different rooms for meetings. The prison authorities allowed this because it made them look good and gave them a certain kind of status. Through these meetings and by the grace of God, thousands of prisoners were set free from the captivity of their addictions and never returned to them.

Behnam also realized that the criminals facing death row for their heinous crimes were the ones very open to salvation. They were addicts with damaged personalities and no future or hope; they had given up. The world had rejected them, but Jesus Christ was waiting for them. It was mainly these that came to Christ in prison, and were also delivered from narcotics and all kinds of addictions.

Despite the trials, brother Behnam also recognized God's many blessings because of the challenges. One of the greatest blessings that God granted him was His own presence. God extended his vision and sight and expanded his world and thinking. The Lord taught him to think like King David did in Psalms 138 where he says, "I walk in trials," and yet he also said, "the kings of the world will know your name." The heavenly dreams Behnam experienced strengthened him in times of trials and kept him from feeling frustrated or disappointed.

Meanwhile, Behnam's wife and children were also facing many trails during his imprisonment. Often, the family of prisoners become more damaged than even the prisoner himself due to the incredible mental pressures they face. These pressures can be financial or simply how one deals with this type of situation. It can be from the embarrassing looks of others, looking down on the family or the disrespect and humiliation of the courts and government related agencies towards the families as they follow processes to fight for their loved ones. And there are some things that just cannot be talked about but leaves a mark that takes much time to heal and recover from.

When a person goes to prison, there is no organization in Iran supporting the prisoner's family. It exists on paper and is advertised as so, but the government does nothing. Behnam's family was no exception. While he was in prison, VEVAK invaded his home again. This scared and shocked his family in such a way that it left his daughter psychologically and mentally damaged, and caused his son to run a fever for a few days following the incident.

Two and a half years before Behnam was to be released, he was asked to report to the prison guard where he was taken immediately to the court and VEVAK office. For eighteen days, no one knew where he was. They began interrogating him and urging him to write a repentance letter. Signing a repentance letter was the only hope he had of getting out early, and he refused to sign it. Without any proof or documentation, they accused him of forming a group to alter the regime. They put him on trial and sentenced him to serve six more years in prison in southeast Iran.

For a political or Christian prisoner, it is the general policy of the Islamic republic to falsely accuse and charge them with new things to prolong their sentence as long as possible. Furthermore, the judge is merely a show during a trial and is powerless. It is VEVAK that decides everything for the judges and every sentence is pre-set before the trial. They do not listen to anything the accused may say, as the trial is merely a formality. This is the kind of injustice that many prisoners face and no one hears their voices.

Behnam appealed the six-year sentence and by the Grace of God, outside pressure from the media, and the exceptional attorney he had, he was exonerated from the charges. Finally, in October of 2016, Behnam was released from the central prison in Karaj.

As wonderful as it was to be with his family again and hug his children, it was also a strange feeling for him, once he was released, because he felt that the whole of Iran was a prison for him. He could not feel free when there was no freedom of worship, a constant feeling of being watched, forbidden fellowship, and even the inability to purchase a Bible from a bookstore. The walls of the prison were really only a prison inside of a prison to him. And yet he also says, "Those walls never imprisoned me… because God was with me."

Due to the enormous pressure placed on believers and the many difficulties Christians in Iran inevitably face, Behnam and his family decided to leave Iran and now live in Turkey.

Many immigrants desire that their children receive a higher education and learn a new language to help build a future for themselves in their new country. Although these things are important, Behnam's priority, vision and hope for his family is to see his children filled with the Holy Spirit, submitted to the Lord and the message of the hour, and ready for the rapture. He says, "I don't think that it's an impossible dream if our hearts are warm with the Lord."

Behnam also desires to see unity amongst believers. After his release, he saw that many different groups had formed within the message, and this has grieved his heart. It is his prayer that the discrepancies can be worked out and unity can be accomplished based upon the Word of God and in Christian love for each other. He was blessed and extremely thankful for the brotherly love that was personally shown to his family through the spiritual and personal support they received from believers outside of their own group during his imprisonment. He says, "My heart is with you. And I pray that all our hearts will be with God. Amen."

CHAPTER 4

A BACKGROUND TO OUR MISSION IN TURKEY

There are currently four established churches in Turkey that are following the Message and attending various Skype services, which we have set up. These churches are in the following cities: Sivas, Eskisehir, Isparta and Denizli (once known as Laodicea). We also have believers across the country in Manisa, Van, Afyon, Ankara, Burdur, Zangolduk, Kayseri and Istanbul.

During my first trip to Turkey in 2011, I was still working full-time, and I was accompanied by Brother Don Hoffman, my wife and a sister in the church. We were working with "The Church of Iran" as they refer to themselves. This group was started by the two brothers who were half-Congolese and they had established the direction of order under the guise of Ewald Frank. Even though Ewald Frank did not know who they were, they were using his name as well as Brother Branham's name. They had set a bishop and council of elders over all the churches in the entire country. Obviously, this system was not in line with Message doctrine. However, the people had no idea since they only had five Messages translated. Regardless, the people have accepted this sort of denominational hierarchy.

When we arrived on the first trip, there were two churches setup under the auspices of the Church of Iran, in Turkey. We visited and met with each church and began to work with them. It became obvious that they had little to no understanding of the Message. This realization renewed our focus to work with the ministers to get them more Message materials and proper teaching of the Message. When I finally heeded the Lord to go full-time into missions and began traveling more often to Turkey, there were three churches under the Church of Iran. My vision at that time was to teach them and help them grow deeper in the Message of the hour.

In August 2012 when I was going to meet with Nehemiah, my translator, in Denizli, the bishop of the Church of Iran said there was a little problem with our trip. I asked what the problem was and he responded that Nehemiah was not authorized to travel. I asked him if it was the Iranian Government at fault. He stated, the Council of Elders did not authorize it. I asked why and was told that Nehemiah was under church discipline. This was news to everyone. The bishop then said they would find another translator for me.

Meanwhile, Nehemiah was already in Denizli fellowshipping with the local church. The believers there had no idea that this structure was in complete violation of the Message. They thought they were doing the right thing. But I also began to realize that the Council of Elders were skilled politicians. I called another brother that was on the council and asked if Nehemiah was under church discipline. He responded that Nehemiah was not and that this was simply not true.

A political debate ensued, amid my efforts to ascertain who would be translating the service that evening. Brother Kourosh, the pastor, preferred Nehemiah translate and I told him that based on the Message of the hour, it was his choice--that he has the final call. However, he felt as though he should not make the call. So, by the time the service started another man was called in to translate. As the pastor began, the translator stepped aside and said that since Nehemiah was in the service, he should translate. The pastor looked at me and asked me what he should do. You could sense the fear he had of the leadership. I told him that he was the pastor and asked him what he wanted to do. He said he would like Nehemiah to translate and Nehemiah came up and proceeded to do so.

From then on, the fury of the bishop came down upon us. One thing or another was going on and in the meantime, all these believers were confused, asking what they should do. To address the issue, I began having small Bible study-like discussions where we talked about subjects like the "Anointed Ones at the End Time," Nicolaitanism, and the sovereignty of the local church. Little by little they began to understand.

We traveled to another city for a couple of days

when the people contacted us and said they had felt the leading of the Lord. They said they were going to break ties with the Church of Iran's system and were excited to work with us instead. I said we would be back in a few days and would then begin some services. When we returned, and sat down with the believers to get some services going, they began backtracking saying they never said they wanted to break ties with the Church of Iran. I confronted them and again they said I was wrong, they had never said that. This culminated in breaking ties between us and the Church of Iran.

Before this trip, I was excited about all that God would do, how God was going to open doors, how He was going to do great things. And then everything that I thought would occur exploded into a fractured and seemingly fruitless effort. I was frustrated; I was disappointed. Announcements on Facebook proclaimed, "Jason is with Satan" and "He's splitting and dividing the church." Following that trip, I had two people that wanted to work with me. That's it: two ministers and no church. To say I was discouraged would have been an understatement.

Upon returning home I thought, well, I guess I should return to my job. One morning shortly after my return home I was having morning devotions. I was contemplating how I should respond and what I should do next. As I went through my daily reading I came across this in the Psalms.

Psalms 109:2-4 For the mouth of the wicked and the

mouth of the deceitful are opened against me: they have spoken against me with a lying tongue. 3 They compassed me about also with words of hatred; and fought against me without a cause. 4 For my love they are my adversaries: but I give myself unto prayer.

Now, I knew what I was supposed to do, pray! Then I went to read the Quote of the Day from branham.org and it said this.

They had seen ten powerful miracles performed down in Egypt: flies, lice, fire, death angel. All they had seen in Egypt. All these great miracles that they'd seen God do, and were still carnal thinkers. And then they saw the Red Sea, that was laying in the path of duty. They were on their road marching then, come out, there was a Pillar of Fire before them, and they marched on to the Red Sea. And when they got there, right in the line of duty laid an obstacle. And first thing you know, fear struck them, and they didn't know what to do. That's the way people does today. When fear strikes them when they're right in the path of duty... Listen, brother, let me say this: If you're walking in the light, having fellowship with God, with His people, and the Holy Spirit is upon you, and you meet an obstacle right in the path of duty, don't stop, just keep pressing on. God will make a way through it. That's one of the greatest experiences of my life, is to see God. When I can't get over it, get under it, get around it, or anyway, God opens up a way and I go through it. Somehow or another His grace is sufficient to carry us through it. [9]

My path was now clear, I felt peace, though I didn't

---

[9] 60-0723 - Speak To The Rock And It Shall Give Forth His Water, Rev. William Marrion Branham, http://table.branham.org

understand everything, and I knew what to do. Pray for those that speak against me and don't be afraid, keep going forward and God will make a way. A few weeks after my return to the States my decision reverberated through the churches in Iran and Turkey. As a result, I received a phone call from a brother named Petros that had just gotten out of prison, having served one year because of his faith. He told me that he wanted to work with me and that God was sending him to Turkey.

Brother Petros

Petros Fouroton was born and raised in a middle class religious family where his mother was a devoted Muslim, but his father was not serious about Islam. As a child, brother Petros was eager to follow the principles of Islam even though he did not know exactly what that meant. He tried to live according to the Islamic manner and teachings and do good for other people, but all the while, there were two opposing powers struggling within him. He grew up in a neighborhood known for all kinds of criminal activities, and at the age of twelve, he started down a destructive path. On one hand, he was looking for God, and yet on the other hand, he believed he found pleasure in his sin.

However, he began to take a closer look at his life and realized that he was not happy in his sin at all. He saw how bad his situation really was and could see no way out of it. He was drowning himself in his sins and mistakes day by day, just like a person being drowned in the sea without knowing it. Everything was vanity and there was no light in his life. His older brother had also been influenced down the wrong road and they had been traveling it together. Slowly brother Petros began to realize that his brother had been changing. His brother did not use harsh language anymore; he was being polite and good; he was helping people in need without others knowing. Brother Petros was surprised by all of this and kept asking himself what had happened to his brother's life that there was such a notable change, until one day he saw his brother take a book from his drawer. It was covered in paper and he could not read the title. His brother would read the book and then put it back in the drawer and lock it. Brother Petros became more and more curious about this book that he was hiding.

Finally, one day brother Petros could contain himself no longer and questioned his brother, "Wait a minute. What has happened to you? What are these things...I cannot make any sense of them? Would you please tell me what has happened to you?"

"What has happened?" his brother responded. But instead of answering brother Petros, he left saying, "We will talk later."

After a while, brother Petros realized that the hidden book was a New Testament. He went to his neighbor and asked him if he knew anything about it. His neighbor said he did and proceeded to tell strange and weird stories about the book that did not even exist in the Bible. Brother Petros again went to his brother asking to know what had happened to him and what was in the book that had changed him. And again, his brother said they would talk about it later as he left once again. Brother Petros and his brother helped their father with his business, and curiously, every day his brother would disappear for a bit and then come back after 30 or 40 minutes.

Brother Petros was so persuasive and insistent to know what was going on in his brother's life that one day, his brother brought a friend over. It was a mutual friend of theirs and after talking for a minute, brother Petros realized with sudden clarity that this friend was like his brother and had also changed. They did not talk for long, but the friend did tell brother Petros one thing; he said, "Whatever we were following up to this point, it was just a lie and not from God. Jesus Christ is the one who can change your life to the point that you won't commit sin anymore." Until that moment, brother Petros had never heard the name of Jesus Christ.

Brother Petros asked, "Are you sure that Jesus Christ can really change my life? Can He really do something that I won't sin anymore? Can he change my personality and give me a new one?"

"He will do it if you want to," the friend responded.

"What should I do?"

"There is nothing you should do; just come and

repent."

So together they went to a dark place down the street where the friend asked brother Petros to sit down that they may pray together. He learned that this was the place that his brother had disappeared to every day to pray. They called it "Desert Church." It was here that brother Petros repented and received Christ as his Lord and Savior at 16 years old.

After coming to Christ, the first thing he and his brother did was to share their story with their family and invite them to Christianity as well. They told their family that if they would just give their hearts to Christ, He could change their lives. However, this went over like a blast in the family; everyone began crying and weeping and asking them why they had made such a decision. Brother Petros' father tearfully pleaded with him, "Son, I smell blood on this road. Don't go down this road please. They will kill you." To see his father crying and begging him to stop was extremely hurtful to brother Petros, but he told his father, "As much as I love you, dad, there is something that I cannot change because He has already changed my life."

Their father waited one day to see if his boys would give up their new way of life. After 24 hours, he told them that since they had chosen this new faith they must leave. They were cast out of the house so quickly that brother Petros did not even have enough time to put on his socks; he had to put them on in the street.

Since brother Petros had never read the New

Testament for himself yet, his brother told him that in it Jesus says to be cheerful and rejoice when people say bad things about you because of Him...that your reward is mighty in heaven. This encouraged brother Petros and increased his joy so much so that he did not care whether he would sleep on a bus or a park bench.

They struggled through the next few days sleeping on the streets. Meanwhile, there was much back and forth going on with their father until he finally relented and agreed to let them back into the house.

It was about a year later that brother Petros was first asked to report to the VEVAK office. At 17 he was not afraid and found it rather exciting. He was told to report in at 9 am, but he overslept and was late to the meeting. When he told the officials, what happened, they asked him what kind of person would oversleep when most people are full of anxiety at such a meeting. Brother Petros told them he could come back another day if they would prefer, but they assured him they would talk to him that day.

When a person is summoned to the VEVAK office, the officials usually try to convince the person that they are wrong and have made a mistake. They play games and provide the person with a document to sign stating that he/she promises to stop attending any more church services. When presented with this, brother Petros signed it twice saying that he would guarantee and promise that he *would* be in the next church service. The officials said he was crazy and out of his mind, but brother Petros told them that it was his decision and that was what he was going to do. They told him he could go but that they would be in further contact with him. He found it to be a tremendous experience to testify of his faith and to be counted worthy to be persecuted for the sake of Christ. Although this was his first summon, it was not to be his last. Time and again he was asked to report in, and each time it was the same. Sometimes he was asked to report somewhere he had never been before to talk to people he had never talked to before. He would sit facing the wall while his questioner would sit behind him and talk to him. On one of these meetings, brother Petros was feeling upset and raised his voice to the official behind him. He asked the official what the reasoning was behind all their questioning since they knew he was not a political activist and simply living out his faith. He told him he was not afraid of them and only wanted to live for God. The only thing the official said in return was that he was crazy and would lose his head one day.

VEVAK became more and more serious in dealing with brother Petros until it eventually escalated into his arrest in 2010. Brother Petros was attending a church service in Shiraz when VEVAK agents suddenly came in and arrested him and 5 other church members. Brother Petros asked for the others to be released since they were only church members and it was him they wanted anyway, and the next day the other 5 were released. However, Brother Petros was handcuffed, blindfolded, and taken to an unknown location where he was interrogated for 2-3 hours before they sent him to a room they called "The Suite." Once he was finally able to take his blindfold off, he introduced himself to the two other men he would share the room with for much of his stay. Hungry, he asked them if they had anything to eat.

They looked at him incredulously and replied, "Aren't you new here? What is wrong with you? How can you be hungry when everyone else loses their appetite from being depressed and under such great stress when they arrive?"

"This is not a problem for me because I knew I would end up here one day," brother Petros responded. He realized that even though he did not enjoy being there, he was there for the work of God and thus, everything would be okay. He was in custody for 54 days, interrogated 37 times, and each interrogation was 8 hours long. During an interrogation, he would face the wall and continually write. He had nothing to hide so whatever they asked he answered with Scripture. Because he had decided to be a Christian and work for the Lord, it was not difficult to answer their questions; the difficulty came when they would ask the same questions over and over.

After 54 days, brother Petros was released on bail. For the next 18 months, he never stopped his ministry. He travelled and continually ministered the Word, spending most of his time in the same town he had been arrested. After 18 months, he was sentenced along with a few others, to one year in prison. Another brother had posted bail for him so brother Petros was going to report to prison. But the others also sentence told him he did not need to do that. They said he did not have a verdict paper in his hand. They said it was not a court order. They said the court would try to keep him for the longest time they could. He was receiving so many calls from all different directions that he finally just turned off his cell phone. He prayed for guidance and felt the Lord was telling him that the same thing that had happened to Joseph would also happen to him; there was nothing to worry about. So, brother Petros went and reported to the prison office that he was there to serve his time.

Once in prison, the difficulties began coming in waves to the point brother Petros was asking God, "Didn't you tell me it would be like Joseph for me? What are you doing then?" Without any reason, VEVAK would call the prison office and ask them to put brother Petros in solitary confinement for a week or so. Also, since the prison officers knew he was a Christian, they would put him in a cell block called "Koran block" where everyone was obligated to read the Koran.

Petros asked them, "I'm a Christian, why are you putting me here in the "Koran block?" But prison official responded and said, "It's ok, you just go and we won't make you read." In prison, he had to deal with many types of psychological pressure. One day he was laying in his bed in the prison cell and they called him to report to the prison office. And when he got to the office they gave him new clothing. This was a certain kind of clothing that they only gave to specific types of inmates.

This was strange for Petros, but what they did was that they blindfolded him, handcuffed him, put shackles on his feet and dragged him out of the prison, then put him into a car and drove off. He began to think, "I came here to serve my time and now where are they taking me." The head of the security services that was with me was using his radio asking, "Hey, open the big gate. Close the other gate. Open the big gate." He would tell the driver to slow down because we were waiting for escort. He was shocked and he kept asking himself where are they taking me, with all these security procedures and without anyone knowing what was going on.

After 20 minutes of driving and hearing them talk on the radio, they took him out of the car. He could see from underneath his blindfold that he was coming out from a shadowy place to a sunny area.

They took Petros to a place he had never been before in his life. It was a new prison, he could hear other inmates screaming and shouting, "Bring this prisoner to my cell! I want him with me!" Another guy would shout, "No. I want him with me in my cell!" Petros was wondering, what kind of place is this? "Did they bring me here to torture me?"

They put him in a cell and didn't even take off his blindfold. After a few minutes, the same inmates that were shouting for him to be in their cells told him VEVAK was gone and he could take off his blindfold. He was so scared he just sat there for a few minutes with all that fear. He took off his blindfold and all he could see was bars and very scary people behind those bars. Cells right next to each other. Things that you could see just in the movies.

"Where did you come from?" was the first question they asked him. He told them he was coming from Adel Abad prison. They told him this is Adel Abad. Petros said, "What are you talking about? They brought me from another place. Are you telling me that we are in the same Adel Abad prison?" They told him, "Yeah this is block number 1 in the same prison." Block number 1 was a place they kept very dangerous serial killers and drug dealers.

They wanted to scare him using psychological torture. The only thing that came to his mind to ask them was is it possible that we cross these bars and see each other? They laughed and said don't worry maybe we can visit each other once a week. He was so relieved and happy that he was not going to deal with these guys daily. They were the kind of people that you do not even want to see them in movies.

After a few days, he asked them what there were there for. He started making conversations, and they told him that they were all on a death row. Petros was there for 11 days. Days kept going by and they kept changing his cell block, and his cells. And for no reason, no excuse, they kept sending him to other places, this was very harsh and difficult.

But, the warden came to him one time and asked him, "how long do you want to go and evangelize people and make us to put you in a solitary confinement?" Petros' response was, "you're been lied to because if I talked with two people about the gospel, other people have come and told me that I talked to twenty people." He then expressed his anxiety and how frustrated he was with his treatment. The warden then said, "I can help you out, I will send you out of this internal core of prison where you can work, so you can be busy and there is no reason for people to tell lies about you."

That was when Petros started to see the fulfillment of God's promise in prison. That was the place that he got in contact with prison authorities. They started talking to him and asking him why he was in prison. Andy he would tell them he is a Christian and here because of his faith. Some of them would say "it's clear to us if you would've said that you're not a Christian, they wouldn't have sent you here."

It might be hard to imagine, but that all those Muslim men admired Petros because he was standing for his faith and what he believed to be the truth. And this was happening every day to a point that the prison authorities could see him working and they would call him over saying, "God bless you and we're proud of you." They really loved him.

One of the prison officers who was really highly ranked among them told Petros "I might not be able to give you time off from prison, but there is one thing I can do. When you're being released from prison, I will get you a plane ticket so you can have a safe journey."

Petros asked him, "Are you serious, you're going to do that for me?" He said, "Yeah, the day that you're being released I will get you a plane ticket so you can have a comfortable journey back home." The same person once told me, "I give you my word. I swear to my honor that I will do my best to get you an early release." He kept his word and was able to get me out of prison one month early.

Present Truth Ministries was working with the website prisoneralert.com regarding Petros' situation and he started to receive letters at the prison from Christians all around the world. He never received any of them before he started establishing a friendship with prison authorities. After that, they gave him four or five letters. They gave him two boxes of chocolates that were sent from United States. They told him that these things are yours. They were many of these things that they threw in the garbage, but these are the remnants and we're going to give them to you.

Prison officials couldn't speak or read English. But there was a guy, they used to call him Mr. Eugenia. He was a close friend of one of the prison authorities. He was responsible for reading Petros' letters. He told me that over and over he begged prison authorities to send him to Petros' cell so he could to talk with him. And they said it is not possible because Petros was a dangerous guy. Mr. Eugenia found the bible that a church member brought to prison for him but was confiscated by the guards.

And his first desire was reading my bible and looking for Petros, to be able to talk to him. He tried his best to come to the inner core of cell blocks to see Petros, but he couldn't make it. But God, brought Petros out of that place so I could meet that man. When he came out this person found him and called him, saying, "Are you Mr. Fouroton?" Petros said, "Yeah." He said, "It has been a long time that I've been looking for you. I want to give my heart to Christ. But before that I want to talk to you."

He brought Petros the New Testament that they used to read and pray together. What God did was keeping His word. Bringing Petros out of that situation. Giving him favor inside the prison with the prison authorities. So, because of that this person was saved. And God fulfilled his Word and it was tremendous.

After he was released from prison, he spent a few months recovering. But after getting out of jail he had a record for "political activities". And as a result, you can't have a normal life with a job or anything like that. And, so he had to leave the country and go to Turkey.

Petros had known Nehemiah in Iran, having met in church. They were friends and used to be a part of the same church. Petros was aware that I was doing missions in Turkey, but had never met me. He was aware that I was spreading the word about his situation while he was in prison. After his release, he spoke on the phone several times with me and as a result ended up going to Turkey and meeting with Nehemiah. They discussed the ministry and things related to the church. That was when Petros, Nehemiah and I extended right hand of fellowship, and started ministering together in Turkey.

Ministering in Turkey wasn't easy to begin with because we were alone and we had to start everything from scratch. Nehemiah and Petros lived together in Eskisehir and the cities that they planted churches in were many hours away, and they took the bus to those cities, sometimes it was 8, 10 or even 20 hours in the bus to have fellowship with people.

When we started our ministry in Turkey, we started it in a city called Sivas, and there was just a couple of families in that town. It was around Christmas time and Petros and Nehemiah decided to hold a Christmas banquet. We always use the Christmas banquet as an opportunity to outreach. And that is when all kinds of people come and they have this opportunity to hear about the message of the gospel.

Something amazing happened during our Christmas service. They held a service at the second floor of McDonald restaurant in Sivas. We didn't have a lot of money and we tried to put our money together so we would be able to provide for this event. We invited roughly 60 people by invitation cards. It was an amazing night because 140 or 150 people showed up. It was a wonderful service and a really good time of worship. Nehemiah spoke about the plan of redemption, starting at Serpent's Seed, told his testimony and as a result, 18 people came to Christ. It was tremendous and God was behind all that they were doing.

After Christmas and during follow ups with these new converts, a few other people gave the heart to Christ as well. By God's grace, we planted the first church in Sivas. It was just the beginning. From Sivas, God opened a door for us to other places in different cities, like Adana which is a very big city.

God really helped us, and we were able to go to different cities, and the work of God was increasing. It was increasing to the point that we kept travelling and we didn't get a chance to get some rest in our own house. That was how the ministry started from scratch to the point we didn't have time to rest in our home town. And God once again, glorified His own name and fulfilled His word.

What Petros feels he is called to do is to introduce many Persian speaking believers to the message of the hour. He doesn't say that he wants to merely talk about the Gospel of Jesus Christ is because there are many other people out there doing that through satellite channels or other means.

But people need to receive a real genuine message from the Lord. The light that God sent through His people in this age to lead them from darkness to light. Petros said, "Of course, I will be more than happy to share the gospel with people as well because there was a time that the gospel was shared with me as well. But my dream and vision is to share the message of God that is sent to this generation through his prophet."

One of the main things in the ministry in Turkey is

for the ministers to be able to spend time with new believers because there are many people willing and desiring to know about the message of the hour. But because there are just a few ministers in the field to talk to them, sometimes the meetings with them must be delayed. Petros is not living in Turkey anymore, he was directed through the UNHCR process to Germany so he needs to travel back and forth from Germany to Turkey.

Traveling back to Turkey, for us, is not an easy thing. There are many things that we go through and there are obstacles for us to be able to come here. There are many things needed for the ministry in Turkey so we can see that God is raising more and more laborers. There are many needs. For example, people need to be able to read Brother Branham's messages for themselves. They need to be able to listen to those messages in their own language.

Petros is extremely gifted in sharing the Message with denominations as well as making contacts and connecting with the people, to share the very basics of the Message with them. When he came to Turkey God led him to the city of Ankara. He was walking down the street when he began a conversation with an Iranian man. He asked the man why he was in Turkey, and the man told him that he and his wife had to flee Iran because they were pastors in the denominational church. He said they were in Turkey going through the UN process and were unsure what to do. Petros began to talk to them about their faith, which led to talking about water baptism, then Godhead and continued with the dangers of denominationalism. As the conversation continued, the brother and his wife were absolutely amazed at what they heard. The man they met was brother Hamed Rezai.

CHAPTER 5

THOSE IMPACTED BY THE MISSION

The other minister, Brother Hamed, was a pastor in Sivas, Turkey. At that time, we still did not have a church established in Turkey. Petros and Nehemiah were the ones I had contact with in Turkey, along with Brother Parviz in another city. Immediately God led Petros to Hamed who became a pastor and was then directed to the city of Sivas by the UN.

Brother Hamed Rezai was born and raised in Tehran, Iran but is now the pastor in the church in Sivas, Turkey. He was considered Muslim-born, as is the custom in Iran, and he was immediately immersed in this religion through his family and education. He followed the religious ceremonies but was never satisfied. He never felt like he could get the proper understanding of the religion because it was always dictated to him and forced upon him whether he was accepting of it or not.

He had many questions including, "Why should I say my prayers to certain directions? Why can't I talk to God? How can we put God, Creator of Heaven and Earth, in a small cubical house in Saudi Arabia?" The latter question he saw as idolatry and he had no desire to worship idols, he wanted to worship God, but he could never find Him or encounter Him. He believed there was a God but that He was unable to be known. For about three years, brother Hamed held an agnostic understanding and view of the universe. He never denied there was a God, but no one was ever able to present God to him so he decided it was God's job to manifest Himself to him.

He believes this is what God was waiting for, because that is exactly what He began to do. God began working and manifesting Himself to brother Hamed. In 2002 or 2003, Brother Hamed was presented with the Gospel and came to Christ in the denominational Pentecostal Protestant church, and two years later was baptized. For nine years, brother Hamed studied many volition teachings and attended different seminaries and conferences. He began working as a minister and served as a supervisor to be a local pastor.

Due to the circumstances in Iran, believers did not have access to different materials, other denominations, or other believers. There was very little fellowship and many people did not even have access to the Word. Because of this limited access, people would join the denominational system and begin to see the system as the definition of Christianity.

Although brother Hamed was a part of this system at the time, there were many things that still did not make sense to him. He had question and ideas that could not be answered because it was not described in Pentecostal theology. They were questions like, "How can God be three different persons?" And, "How can there be different kinds of sin in God's sight? Sin is sin so it shouldn't matter if we have good sin or bad sin." Or, "Jesus teaches us to stay away from denominations and organizations and yet we belong to one." His pastor's answer to this last thought was that even though they were a denomination, they were the most perfect and best denomination. This reasoning did not make sense to brother Hamed. In his mind, denomination was denomination.

Despite these questions, he dedicated himself to learning and growing in all that he could and taught others what he had learned. But eventually, he came to a place where the theology was not enough anymore. He had a hunger for more of God and believed there was more to be had, but he could not find the answers to satisfy his hunger.

This deep desire led him to begin praying and asking God to send him wherever God wanted him to go. He felt like God was leading him to Turkey, but he resisted this nudge time and again, even while he continued to pray for the Lord's will to be done.

He tried to find another city with a Pentecostal church where he could fellowship and was offered positions to minister in different Pentecostal churches, but the harder he tried to make this work, the more the Lord closed the doors.

Brother Hamed recalls praying one day and remembered the story of Jonah and how Jonah told the Lord that he would do whatever God wanted him to do. Yet, when God told Jonah to go to Nineveh, Jonah went in the opposite direction instead, contrary to the will of God. Brother Hamed thought, "There is no difference between me and Jonah right now. I have been asking for the will of God and He is telling me to go to Sivas, Turkey, but I am trying not to go there." Then the Lord reminded him of Matthew 28:19, "Go and preach the gospel and make them disciples." Once he realized he was supposed to bring the Gospel to the people and make them disciples, he could move forward in God's will for him.

God gave brother Hamed the strength to leave the country, but when he finally arrived in Sivas, Turkey, he was not happy to be in a city without any church or any fellowship. However, the Lord directed him to Brother Nehemiah and brother Petros and they began to fellowship together. They talked about many subjects, doctrines and questions that had gone unanswered in Hamed's mind, and the brothers answered them according to the Scripture. It was as if God had opened brother Hamed's ears and removed the veil from his eyes, and he could finally see the reality of the Scripture. His hunger was being satisfied and it was sweet to his soul.

As wonderful as this new revelation was, he still struggled to put away worldly living and to go against his flesh to have deeper fellowship with the Lord. And yet, he considered it a "Sweet Suffering."

Today he testifies that God sent a vindicated prophet, and that God is present today and dwelling in His church. God wants him to be a loyal and faithful Virgin Bride, ready to meet his heavenly Bride-groom, Jesus Christ, and enter that wedding ceremony with Him. He is so grateful to know the reality and truth of the message and believes as the Scripture says, "I chose you before the foundation of the world to be blameless in love." He knows it is God's grace that God loves him regardless of his past sins and chose him to be likened unto Christ so that he can love those around him as well.

Sivas is a city that had not had a church there for almost 1,400 years and is a mix of Afghans and Iranians. Hamed decided to send out an invitation, inviting everyone, including Muslims, to a Christmas service and banquet. Nehemiah gave his testimony and introduced the plan of salvation, beginning with the serpent seed doctrine. By the end of this service 18 people came forward and gave their hearts to God. This was the beginning of the first church in Sivas.

In January, we rented a little room for the services in Sivas and continued to bring the gospel to Muslims. Another five people came to Christ during that trip. We also spent time with Hamed and his wife, Sister Nasim, bringing to them the testimonies of the vindication of Brother Branham's ministry since they were still new to the message.

Brothers Nehemiah and Petros were living in

Eskisehir and began an outreach among the Muslims and denominations. With many people coming to the services, it seemed prudent to begin a church in Eskisehir. The next time I returned, there were two churches established. We mainly had evangelistic services to explain the gospel and get the people saved and into the baptism of the Holy Ghost. These were amazing and exciting services to be a part of. This was the first opportunity I had experienced, to lead a Muslim to Christianity.

Brother Siamak

During the time of ministry in Eskisehir, Nehemiah and Petros met with a young man deeply struggling with addiction.

Brother Siamak Azadi was born into a very serious and intellectual Muslim family. His parents took reading and studying very seriously. His brothers were protestors in politics and government. Interestingly enough, their personal home library also had some books about Christianity including a New Testament, *A Guide to the New Testament*, and *A Man on The Cross*. Sometimes these books would catch Brother Azadi's attention and he would desire to read them. But then he would think, "How can Islam be wrong? It's apostasy to even think about it. I was born a Muslim and I should honor it and not betray my God." He never knew who put these books in their library as they were serious Muslims, but looking back he realized his heavenly Father used these books to begin his work in his life and to bring it to maturity.

As a teenager Azadi was very interested in Farsi literature and poems. He quickly realized he had a gift in this area and began studying Farsi literature and writing his own material. His thirst to know more about God caused him to predominantly write literature praising his god and the prophet of Islam. It was not long before he made a name for himself in Farsi literature as well as having obtained a good job in the that field. His fame surrounded him with new people and he began smoking, drinking, using drugs and living an adulterous lifestyle. He still considered himself a Muslim, thirsty for God but continued doing whatever he desired, drowning in sin.

As time went on, he suddenly lost his job without any explanation. He found another job working for the government and again he lost that job, as well, without any explanation. To make matters worse, he was dismissed from the university he was attending. He finally realized that his brother's political activities had caused him to be placed under surveillance, despite his opposition to his brother's views.

When he was about 20 years old, his brothers had suggested he leave the country to live a safe life without constant surveillance: he fled to Turkey. However, being a drug addict led him to begin dealing in drugs as soon as he arrived in Turkey. In no time, he became a monster whose only goal was to make money no matter the consequences. He quickly became one of the largest dealers, smuggling drugs from Iran to Turkey, forging documents and dealing in human trafficking in Istanbul. Because of his years of addiction, he used every type of drug available and they became his god. Money allowed him to immerse himself in immorality. He was arrested and imprisoned several times and at one point, spent more than 6 years in prison. In and out of prison became the rhythm of his existence.

The last time he was arrested he was placed in custody for 27 months, without a trial. It was during this time that he began thinking about God again. He began fasting and praying to the god of Islam once again. However, the more he tried to progress, the less he achieved; he became frustrated and hopeless.

His brother, a convert to Christianity, suggested that he pray in the name of Jesus. Brother Azadi thought this was ridiculous but did not say anything to his brother, out of respect for him. But he had had a cellmate that was Muslim, and every time brother Azadi mocked his brother and his faith his Muslim cellmate would say, "Don't do that. I have seen many miracles among Christians and in the church. You should have respect." And every time he just laughed at him.

A short time later, his brother asked him to read the *New Testament* and this time Azadi became upset with his brother for questioning his belief system. As the days went by, he began to talk to this other God, the

Christian God. He said, "If you are God and could save my brother who was deeply involved in addiction and all kinds of things like I am and he has a new life, as he says, then help me and deliver me from this prison;" this time he finished the prayer with: "in the name of Jesus."

After a time, he was called to another trial. The night before, he began thinking of his previous records and all the records with fake names and knew the authorities would not go easy on him. He knew he would have to spend at least a few years in prison. His brother called to tell him he had prayed for him, and again Azadi simply laughed. His Muslim cellmate also told him that he had prayed for him in the name of Jesus and had asked for his freedom. He said, "I have a feeling you will walk away today, but promise that you will turn your life around and live for him." Azadi laughed again and said, "Of course."

At the trial the judge asked brother Azadi to stand as he announced the verdict. Azadi looked at his attorney and his attorney lowered his head in defeat, believing there was no hope for him this time.

The judge said, "You are free to go."

Azadi could not believe his ears. He asked the guard standing next to him, "What is the verdict again?"

"You are a free man," the guard said in a thick Turkish accent.

Azadi looked to his attorney in disbelief. His attorney was also in shock and requested written proof of the verdict. Once Azadi read the verdict, he began to realize he was free. He kept telling himself, "I am lucky to walk away considering my criminal record." He gave no thought regarding his prayers and the prayers of his cellmate and family. Within minutes, he was already planning to find some drugs and get back into business, before he made it through the prison gates.

He walked back to his cell and as soon as he entered, his cellmate said, "I have packed your things. You are set to go, but remember the promise you made this morning: change your life and live for God."

With a bad attitude Azadi replied, "If there was a God and your Christ could do something, He would do it for you so you wouldn't spend all these years here. Stop directing your nonsense at me."

After a few moments of silence his cellmate replied, "I will have my family help you with some funds to get you back on your feet again."

Being a foreigner, he had to go to the foreigner's department at the central police station in Istanbul and remain in custody for the night while they checked his paperwork and verified his residency. He was so glad to be free that he could not sleep most of the night. Around 4 in the morning, he finally went to bed and began thinking about what his brother and cellmate had told him about Jesus, his miracles, and about Him being the Lord. "Nonsense," he concluded and fell into a deep sleep. Soon after, he saw a great light coming closer and closer to him and then heard a mighty voice say to him, "Do not mock your God." It felt like someone then picked him up from the bed and threw him to the floor. Severe pain shot through his back and he began screaming. Everyone in custody was awakened by his screams and came to him. He could not open his eyes; they kept slapping him because he kept shouting from the pain and fear. He cried, "Don't touch me!"

He could not move from the severe pain in his back and within minutes he was sent to the hospital in an ambulance. When he told the doctors that he could not move, they just laughed saying there was no way that his back had been injured from falling off the bed. However, after taking some X-Rays and tests, they concluded that his hip was broken in three places. Due to the nature of his injury, there was no possibility of performing surgery; they told him he would be paralyzed in his left leg for the rest of his life.

After the incident, he began using drugs again and resumed his life as drug dealer and human trafficker. But this time, what had happened that morning was always on his mind and he could not understand it.

Azadi was living in frustration and his brother kept asking him to visit a church to be prayed over, to be healed and delivered from his addictions. His brother had many contacts among churches and Christians believers. He put him in contact with two ministers in Istanbul. Each time they planned to meet one another, something would come up and the meeting would be cancelled. Azadi, not being able to walk, became frustrated and upset with his brother because of several cancellations.

A short while later, he was sent to a small town in Turkey called Eskisehir. His brother, again, tried to put him in contact with a protestant church in town; but for some reason, this time, Azadi refused to go. A week later his brother said he contacted another church through Facebook and someone would contact him soon. Since it was already set up, Azadi could not refuse, even though he was heavily drugged due to his pain.

Another week went by. A man called and introduced himself as Brother Petros and they set up a meeting. He came with another man, Brother Nehemiah, and they listened as Azadi briefly referenced his past. The brothers set up some follow up meetings and gave him a booklet to read. After that they asked him to join them in worship.

This was a new chapter in Azadi's life. With the help of the pastors and all the prayers of the believers, his pain was getting less and less and he began to have a new outlook. He realized that is was God himself, planning everything from the very beginning, for him to be there amongst a small group of believers. He realized that God had directed his every step to keep him free from denominationalism, so he could directly receive the truth of the word.

Step by step, prayer after prayer, Azadi began to feel more convicted about his life. He desired to live a clean life and take a respectable job for a living. One night, heroin in one hand and methamphetamine in the other, he prepared to use them, as usual, when 2 Corinthians 6:2 began replaying in his mind, *For he saith, I have heard thee in a time accepted, and in the day of salvation have I succoured thee: behold, now is the accepted time; behold, now is the day of salvation.* For several hours, he sat there reflecting on all that God had done for him and how God had brought him to where he was now. He thought about losing his ability to walk and how God had a perfect plan in that, as well. He could not stop weeping as he contemplated God's hand in his life. He became determined to change his lifestyle and mustered the strength to flush the drugs down the toilet.

Not long after, fear and anxiety hit him. As an addict, he knew that he would need drugs in a few hours so he continued to read 2 Corinthians 6 through, to the end of the chapter. He believed that his calling was to serve the Lord, and assured himself that God would honor his step of faith and not leave him alone. He closed his eyes and went to sleep with a revitalized faith. That very same night he was delivered from his addiction and never felt the desire for drugs again.

Physically, he was getting better each day, to the point where he began walking on both feet as normally as before the crippling incident. The doctors were confounded at this development. Even recently, he needed a doctor's report and when they were done checking him over, they could not believe he had suffered from a broken hip. There was no sign of it at all in his x-rays.

Everything changed. He stopped smoking and detested drinking. 2 Corinthians chapter 6 was all he could think of, Be ye not unequally yoked together with unbelievers: for what fellowship hath righteousness with unrighteousness? and what communion hath light with darkness?

By God's grace and with the help of his pastor, a year later he started ministering for the Lord as a song leader in his local church. After nearly a decade, his family who had abandoned him during his trials came to visit him. They were amazed as they saw the hand of God in his life. The criminal drug dealer they once knew was now a changed man, standing in a pulpit talking about God and his plan: about love and hope in him, that he, himself, is a living testimony that God is alive and is the same yesterday, today and forever.

He now knows full well why they had a *New Testament* in their library back in Iran, why he was always interested in it and why he lost his health to regain it once again. The things which are impossible with men are always possible with God.

His journey is not yet complete, however. Though he went through many more trials and faced weakness, the Lord never failed him. He had been approved by the UNHCR to resettle in the United States or Canada, but the Lord redirected him. In his own words, he says, *He directed me and told me to leave and I did it. He took me through woods and seas. I faced death and fear and saw many that lost their lives. But I trusted him as he told me to leave Turkey, with one scripture in Joshua, 'Have not I commanded thee? Be strong and of a good courage; be not afraid, neither be thou dismayed: for the LORD thy God is with thee whithersoever thou goest.'*

He finally arrived in Germany and began to work with Petros. Although the devil tried to thwart them in many ways, by God's grace they began to witness to people and denominational believers about the work of God in this age through a vindicated prophet. He considered this a great privilege. The Lord worked in a mighty way and used them to plant the first Farsi speaking message church in Germany and Europe to share the message of the hour with all Farsi speaking people.

Brother Azadi says, I, who was a fisher of souls for the devil, am now a fisher of souls for the kingdom of God. They have a small congregation in Hamburg, Germany that belong to God. Of them he says, God is always manifested in simplicity, but in full strength among us.

CHAPTER 6

THE WORK PROGRESSING IN TURKEY

In early 2013, I returned to Turkey and our efforts blossomed into the establishment of another Message assembly in southern Turkey in the city of Adana. Unfortunately, we had around 45 people in the assembly that left the Message and were attending denominational churches. The bishop of the Church of Iran convinced the denominational pastor in that city to ostracize us, to defeat the work in Adana. About 35 people walked away from the church and from the Message. We know that God is in control of all things, and we would rather have one believer in a city that was serious about the message than large numbers of people.

With the ten-remaining people, we went through the Godhead as well as the history of the church ages to begin to plant the seed of God's ministry through his messenger, Brother Branham. We led some Muslims to faith during this trip and encouraged their stand.

There was a husband and wife in their seventies who had been Muslims all their lives and wanted to hear the gospel. We had just had a full day of meetings and fellowship from 8 am to 11 pm so we asked if tomorrow would work for us to come to their house and talk with them. However, they insisted that they wanted to hear it right then. So, we went to their home at about 11:30 pm and for two hours shared the gospel and answered all their questions. Both the husband and the wife said they wanted to repent and obtain salvation, right then. We gladly prayed with them, and then they asked if they would be executed immediately upon returning to Iran. We assured them that that was very unlikely, but they responded that they were ready to go if they were to be executed. It was wonderful to hear such a stalwart confession of their newfound faith.

I returned to Turkey in October 2013 and right before the trip I had had pneumonia. The Lord quickly delivered me from it, affording me the ability to proceed with the itinerary, but I continued to have a very bad cold throughout the entire trip. I knew the devil was striking because I was drawn to go deeper into the Message with the ministers and with the people. Nehemiah had already taught them the basics of Malachi 4, but I felt very strongly the pull of God to go into Daniel 12 and Revelation 5 and to discuss Revelation 10 and the opening of the 7 seals. For many of the ministers, Nehemiah being the exception, it was the first time they had heard this and were stricken by it. Until then, they had been following Ewald Frank's teachings that the seventh angel of Revelation 10:7 is for Israel. As they began to hear the truth, they were amazed and many questions arose. We continued to follow up with them as they caught the true Revelation.

I arrived once again in February of 2014. Nehemiah had started doing a PowerPoint called, "What is the Message?" It was originally designed by Brother Ron Millevo, but Nehemiah and I added several new things to the presentation and brought it to the various churches in Turkey. We visited a few believers in the city of Trabzon, a city in northeastern Turkey, in the province of Trabzon along the Black Sea coast, and helped them to start meeting together to learn about and understand the Message. I spent a lot of time going through the doctrines of law and grace and their relationship to the law in the new covenant.

Nehemiah and Petros were introduced to a man named Alireza who was a Christian and they immediately began introducing him to the message of the hour.

Brother Alireza

Brother Alireza Raisitoosi is a brother in the Lord, born in Mashhad, Iran who is in his late 40's. It has been six years since he received Jesus Christ as his Lord and Savior. If you were to ask him about his salvation, he would say, "I was actually born six years ago when Christ the Lord changed my whole life, from a curse to a blessing."

Brother Alireza was born into a practicing Islamic family. His mother taught him the laws of Islam and he had a hunger to know this God and his ways; however, they were always struggling financially and he had to work from an early age. He worked very hard to prove himself and to be better than anyone else. At times, he worked up to 20 hours per day. Because of the horrible experiences of his life, he turned to drugs thinking they would give him strength to work harder, while mentally escaping his circumstances. He thought drugs would help him forget his problems and misery. Ultimately, he was looking for peace.

After years of hard work, he finally accomplished what he was striving for. He had begun making good money, he had a good house, a good car and was traveling overseas. Yet something was still missing-- something was wrong somewhere. He delved deeper into drug addiction, though he claimed to love God. He thought that all he needed was God in his life and then he would obtain even more. Sadly, the more he called on God, the more he found himself far from him. None of his prayers were being answered: never once.

During this period in his life, Christian shows began broadcasting and many people were watching them. Alireza began to watch them from time to time. Each time he would get upset, thinking the Christians were infidels and apostates and yet he felt compelled to continue watching. The things they were saying made perfect sense and he would find himself listening for hours and hours. It bothered him when he heard them say, "you can have a relationship with God." He thought, "Why can't I have a relationship with him if this be true?"

He was desperately looking for God but could not find Him anywhere in his life. He became so utterly frustrated that he decided to take his own life. He thought that by doing this he would at least find out if God is real and finally have his questions answered. He decided he must do it, even if his destination would be hell.

It was 2:30 AM when he went to his balcony to have his last smoke of the day. Cursing God, he said, "How can you be God when you don't answer my prayers? Tonight, I will prove to you and myself if you are real or not, by throwing myself down from here. We will see if everything will end after I die and that you don't exist."

Before he had gone out for his smoke, he had been watching a fashion show on TV and had brought the remote out to the balcony with him. He decided to go back in to see his wife one last time and when he walked back in, the TV was on a Christian channel replaying a show from two years earlier. The man on the show was saying, "I know you want to take your own life tonight. God has heard your prayers and wants to enter your life."

Immediately Alireza found himself on his knees crying and saying, "Who am I to have God in my life? I am a sinner." But he repeated a prayer with the TV preacher and received Christ as his Lord and Savior. That day he had used 7 grams of opium; but the moment he repented he told himself, "I will not use this poison anymore, for my God is the almighty God and will change my life!"

His wife hated drugs and hated to see him addicted, but when he told her what had happened she said, "Perhaps you were under the influence and hallucinating. You can't just cut your dose. It is insanity and will take your life."

"No problem; I want to go down this road," he told her.

He suffered severe pain and sickness for two months but he never craved opium again. God delivered him from that bondage. After a year of seeing the change in Alireza's life, his wife came to Christ. Subsequently, her mother accepted Christ as her Lord and Savior as well.

Alireza left Iran and went to Turkey. He began attending an Assemblies of God church. However, it was more like a fashion club than a church. He was looking for a way to know God and his ways so he began searching. His search led him to a church in Eskisehir where Brother Nehemiah was preaching the Message of the hour. With no biblical background, Alireza found himself confused with what he was hearing. He thought, "These men are like Muslims, and why does Christianity have thousands of directions?" But he was sure of one thing, God is a living God and He would lead him in the right direction.

People had been telling him that he should join a Pentecostal church because he had received Christ through a Pentecostal TV show. Some people said many bad things about Message believers and the minister, saying they were frauds and preaching legalism. Alireza struggled in his mind over these things until brothers Nehemiah and Petros invited him to Eskisehir for a visit. They talked about serpent seed and the error of the trinity. Alireza thought, "I am entering the depth of the Scripture now." Through these brothers and the Message of the hour, he truly began to know his God.

After his meeting with them, he was invited to meet a theologian, a brother in Ankara. This brother told him that he was wrong and tried to discredit what brothers Nehemiah and Petros were teaching. Alireza asked the man, "Would you please show me two scriptural witnesses for the trinity? The brothers you speak of proved everything by the scripture so here is your chance."

"The trinity is a mystery and you should simply believe in it," the theologian responded.

To the brother Alireza said, "There is nothing hidden from sons of God because knowing the secrets of the kingdom has been given to them. As Nehemiah suggested, I will kneel before God and ask for His leadership to lead me to the truth." And because he did just that, he fell in love with God. Two years later he knows he could give his life for the Lord in a heartbeat, if that were to be required of him.

When he first came to Christianity, he would invite brothers to visit him and they would say that they would pray and come when God would lead them to come. He thought they were just showing off like Muslim clergies. But now that he has had personal experiences with God, he understands what it means to pray and walk with God wherever he leads and this has changed his life.

Once brother Alireza accepted Christ, it was not easy. In fact, he faced many financial and spiritual trials. But he knew that his heavenly father is the King of Kings and that He would lead him in the direction he should go. He was uneducated and unfamiliar with technology, computers or even smart phones. However, the Lord led him to the United States wherein just 8 months he could get 3 certificates in his work field, get a wonderful job as a chef in a Marriot Hotel, and was blessed both financially and spiritually.

Brother Alireza finishes his testimony with, "Obedience is the greatest thing I have learned from the Lord. Living for him and dying for him is the only goal in my life and I pray that one day I can serve Him. I pray that each one of you meets the King of Kings and God of all beauty, the Lord Jesus, and be His Spotless Bride.

Ministers Meetings

We had our first ministers' meeting in Eskisehir, Turkey in the summer of 2014 and this was a very difficult meeting. There were several people who seemed uncommitted so we decided to strike hard on the teachings of the Message. Nehemiah went into: "What is the Message?" I spoke about modesty and holiness to the Lord; looking at it scripturally, historically and from the Message. We also brought out how Brother Branham in the "Church Ages" sermons talks about receiving the spirit, the baptism of the Holy Ghost, and the new birth.

The Question & Answer session that followed proved which ministers were genuine and sincere in their desire to understand the Message and which ones were distant observers. As difficult as this was, God used it for good to help us understand and direct us on how to move forward, and which brothers could really be trusted to work with.

When I went back to Turkey in October, I talked about the new birth, the Millennium, what salvation is, and about knowing the day of their visitation. We also met with Shahin, the pastor in Denizli. Parviz was the previous pastor before he left and went to Canada. Shahin had been a minister for about 17 years in the Church of Iran when he decided to break ties with them and come and work with us. The first time we met him we realized he had no idea what the Message is. He knew about Malachi 4:5-6, but not its significance. We asked if he knew that Brother Branham condemned having a bishop over a group of churches and he said he did not know this. We continued to share more with him, and he sat with his mouth hanging wide open, in complete shock at what he was hearing.

We have worked with Shahin for a year now. He is

on fire for this Message and says that he has learned more about the Message in the past year than he did in the last 17 years combined.

Brother Shahin

Shahin is now living in Denizli, Turkey, but is originally from Rasht, Iran. He was in born and raised in a Muslim family, and came to Christ in 1997. When he read the Bible, he realized the reality of salvation. Because in Islam there are many things that he heard about but never saw them in practice or in action; in his family or in the people around him. And all you see is because of a religious life in people; without knowing what the truth is, without knowing why they need salvation. And they just follow the principles that they think will lower their burden on judgement day in the presence of Allah. The Bible was the only book that answered every question regarding God and His personality when reading it. That was how he came to Christ.

And he started practicing his faith in a house church back in his home country in Iran. The Assemblies of God was the only church that was in the city that he was living in. And there were not many people attending these services at that time. The best thing that happened to him in the very early days of his Christian walk was being introduced to the message of the hour and brother Branham's ministry. And in fact, it was one of the greatest challenges of his life, choosing between a formal church and a house church.

From the very beginning when he heard about what God did brother Branham's ministry, there was something that was pulling me toward him. After a while he started preaching to people, and they started coming forward to receive Christ. Also, the pressures from the government and other churches started to increase.

Reading through whole Bible we can understand that there's always a hatred towards the children of God, wherever the work of God is being manifested. And in Muslim countries they are against these kinds of activities and consider them an act against their regime. Nevertheless, God answered his prayers and opened many doors for the church. Many souls were being saved and many prayers were answered.

And in fact, but this was all the calm before the storm. In 2005 Mohammad Khatami stepped down as President and Mahmoud Ahmadinejad was elected, as a result pressure against Christians and all minorities in the country increased. And from that time forward security agency called them to report to VEVAK's office telling them to stop their activities, and abandon Christianity. It was first informal suggestions they made trying to make them afraid in order that they would stop all their activities.

After having Mohammad Khatami, a reformer as President, to show a better appearance of Iran amongst world leaders, now there was a more conservative, religious fanatic for President. Before Ahmadinejad there was more freedom regarding politics and journalism and even religion. But after Ahmadinejad took office, there was an increase of pressure on the church and on political activities.

Maybe many people don't know about this truth but let me tell you something; what we're sharing in this book is real people's life experiences and not merely a story. Back in 1995 there was a serial killer, working for the government, that murdered several church leaders. When you come to Christ, as a Muslim, you know that according to Sharia Law you are to be executed.

But for eight years under Khatami they had an open door to evangelize and spread the Gospel. But after that the security services started to open threaten their life. But every time the ministers would give the same answer that they could not stop what God has called them to do and we will continue. And because of this persecution they changed their approach and began to have more small house churches instead of gathering together in a large worship service.

When VEVAK saw, them doing the work of God, evangelizing and sharing the gospel with people, they started to increase their pressure on believers and church leaders. And time after time, they were brought into custody in VEVAK's offices. They started to interrogate them and question them, trying to get them to renounce their faith. Shahin's house was raided by VEVAK on many instances. They used to come and take all his Christian materials; his bible, his booklets, and even his illustration posters; everything he had.

In 2006, there was a nationwide crackdown against our church put in place by VEVAK. Ministers all around the country were arrested and put in prison. To get out of prison they were asked to post bail. The bail was way over their capacity and they could not provide it easily. And we were constantly requesting that they expedite the process because they wanted an answer to know what they were facing; and every time they refused. They received the verdict and sentencing after four years. They were sentenced to a five-year suspended sentence, meaning that if they discontinued their Christian activities they would never have to serve any time in prison. Shahin was one of them.

Meanwhile, VEVAK would keep calling them and telling them to stop their operations. They wanted us to stop everything. But they knew that they were not called to obey a man but to follow the Lord. There was something that was in the heart of all the ministers, and in unity they carried on with their ministry. This led to another VEVAK crackdown later. And with the first suspended sentencing they had, no trial was needed to put them behind bars.

In 2009 Shahin was arrested again by VEVAK and it was at this same time that Youcef Nadarkhani was arrested and shortly after that time was sentenced to death for apostasy. Because of the global pressure on the Iranian government they had no choice but to drop the charge of apostasy against him. Seeing all these things made Shahin think about how can I take my family out of this country; he is married to sister Maryam and has two children, and therefore he decided to leave the country to live in Turkey.

It's not easy to leave the place that you were born and raised, where you have all your ties, your family, and everything there. There were people talking inside of Turkey and saying there was a pervasion in the doctrine of the message of the hour with the group that I was working with. Since Shahin has always been desirous of the truth it was very interesting and somewhat exciting for him to hear about. Because all those who were introduced to the message in Iran, came to the message through the testimony of Ewald Frank from Germany.

In fact, most of what they heard, and read in the church was material from Ewald Frank. And his arrival in Turkey was around the same time that brother Nehemiah and I made another mission trip to Turkey. We met each other and started talking. That was when he could see himself getting closer and closer to the reality of the teaching of the message of the hour. And he could see the perversion that the church he was a part of in Iran was walking into with disregarding the teaching of brother Branham.

Almost every sentence that he was hearing about the teaching of the message of the hour was completely new to him. And today, unfortunately, you can see this pervasion in the message world at some level. Some people who hear the message through brother Branham take only the portions that suit their agenda.

Shahin finally had the opportunity and privilege to

hear about the Son of Man ministry coming of Christ. This renewed his strength and now he had access to more materials; and he could read for himself and go through them.

He had no idea about Revelation 10:7. He had no idea about 1 Thessalonians 4:16. He had no idea about the Mighty Angel. He had no idea that these things are the very foundations of the message. Shahin says, "To me this is what identifies the message of the hour."

At the time of the writing of this book Shahin has been in Turkey for 35 months. He's glad that as time goes by he is hearing and learning new teachings from the message and he's growing in his understanding.

From the very beginning, what motivated Shahin to keep going forward was the voice of God. He could hear the Lord telling him to "move forward and I'll go and open the doors for you." Before he left Iran to come to Turkey, God spoke to him in few dreams. Every time in his dream, he would see himself in a church service and people were there to hear the message. He was rejoicing sitting in a corner of the church just to listen to the service. But after the song service was over, the song leader would call his name and would announce that for today's message we're going to hear the word of God from brother Shahin. It was a dream that repeated a few times. And at the time he was still in Iran and he was struggling with the thought of leaving.

Shahin's vision now is to minister souls so that they can hear the message of the hour as it really is. Shahin says that, "Meeting with Present Truth Ministries missionary team provided me the opportunity to first grow in my own understanding and then provide the materials for the believers so that now they can have access to brother Branham's messages for themselves, and they can read what the message is all about."

Turkey is a very good filter in which you can really separate those real believers with those fake believers with masks that just want to take advantage of Christianity and the opportunities that comes with it. Many churches are preaching liberal Christianity and a modern version of Christianity, and that's what the people like to hear. They don't feel any pressure if they're not modest in those services. They have no obligation to follow the principles of the Lord described in His Word in their lives. And to consider the gospel of Christ and the kingdom of God only as a love of Christ and Christian love.

Shahin states, "But we know that the message delivered to us through a vindicated prophet is pointing us back to the restoration of the Word. And this revelation challenges people; those who surrender themselves and are ready to receive this revelation. And there is a great chance, for sure, they will receive a lot of pressure from the world, but that's when they can show whether they are ready to walk the Lord and in the opposite direction of the world. And I can say this is a difficulty of the work of God on earth. And today I just hope and desire to be useful in this work of the Lord."

Shahin is married to Sister Maryam and has a wonderful testimony of how the Lord touched her life and strengthened her to take her stand for Christ during persecution

Sister Maryam

Sister Maryam, 37, was born in Rasht, Iran. At 20 years old, she accepted Christ only a few months after hearing the message of the Gospel. The more she read the Bible, the more she realized the reality of it. She shared her new faith and excitement with her sister because she wanted her sister to experience the same thing. Together they shared a Bible, but their father was against it. He would get very upset if he saw the sister reading the Bible, so sister Maryam would run to the yard and begin praying for her sister. Sister Maryam would read the Bible in the kitchen or other places her father did not like to be, so her Bible was covered with cooking oil.

It was not until her husband that she became in contact with the church in Iran. Having been raised in a Muslim family, being in a church, singing songs, praying in Farsi, and seeing ministers reading the Bible, preaching and ministering the Word was a new experience for her. Although sister Maryam's husband had been sharing the Gospel with people a year before they had gotten married, it was not until a year after their marriage that they began their own ministry together as a family. They began inviting people to their little apartment to share the Gospel with them, and sister

Maryam would try to serve them with even the smallest things while they were listening. A year later they began holding church services in their home, and two years after that VEVAK began their interrogations. Sister Maryam was interrogated only once, but her husband was called over and over.

The first time VEVAK raided their home, a few men knocked on the door and said they were from the revolutionary court with a search warrant and wanted to come in. When sister Maryam asked them to come back when her husband was home, they said they could not wait and came in. They confiscated everything in the house including picture frames, wedding photos, wedding videos, their Bibles, and even a small Bible for their daughter. At first sister Maryam was angry, but then she remembered that those that followed Christ would be persecuted for His name. She could rejoice in this present persecution and as VEVAK was leaving she told them, "You might confiscate everything and take them away, but there is one you cannot take, and that is Christ within me."

The next day sister Maryam was asked to report to VEVAK's office where they proceeded to question her and then continued to make death threats on her and her husband's lives, saying they would make it look like an accident. Amidst all these difficulties, fears, and anxieties, she was reminded of Psalm 23. God is her Shepherd; she shall not want. This was her first experience and testimony of faith with VEVAK, but it only gave her more boldness as a Christian. From then on, every time she or her husband were asked about their faith, they would explain four things to them: yes, they were Christians; every person has a right to know what Christianity is; we can provide you with the material; and you need the New Testament for yourself.

During the six years of holding services in their apartment, sister Maryam's husband was arrested twice. Sister Maryam was so worried about how her in-laws would handle it if they found out about his arrests. Also, her daughter had begun to talk and kept asking where her daddy was and when he would be coming back. VEVAK finally forbade them to have any more services, and they were compelled to listen to them. They could not afford to buy a house for themselves, but miraculously, her father-in-law received a house through his company. Without even asking, her father-in-law transferred it into sister Maryam's husband's name and gave the house to them. They decorated it nicely and began having services once a week very secretly under the guise of family visits.

Meanwhile, sister Maryam's husband had no job security. He worked for a company that required him to work until 7 in the evening even though their services began at 5pm. As a result, he resigned and began to look for another job. After much searching, he decided to buy a car and became a cab driver.

Being Christian born was also difficult on their daughter. At school, she was required to go to Koran classes and say the prayers. Although her parents explained to the teachers that they were Christians and that their daughter did not know anything about Sharia law, they still forced her to participate in group prayer. They said that if she missed prayer 3 times, she would fail her classes and be cut from the school.

Things progressively got worse in Iran. Sister Maryam's husband told her that he could not tolerate it anymore, but sister Maryam could not imagine leaving and being separated from her family. Meanwhile, her husband was having dreams where he saw himself ministering to groups of people, and every time he shared his dreams with sister Maryam, something pushed them forward. They began to see that even thought they had a little place of their own, they were not able to fellowship with other brothers and sisters. They also began to have more significant difficulties with their families due to their faith, and eventually were forced to leave Iran.

Sister Maryam had never been to Turkey before and was unsure as to what to expect. However, after arriving, she became thankful for the freedoms they now had. She did her best to keep moving forward and to help people wherever she could. One other blessing that came from moving to Turkey was a greater revelation of the message of the hour. She and her husband had known about the message and were familiar with concepts of it, but not in the full reality of it. After meeting with me, sister Maryam was surprised at what she heard and began asking herself what could be in the message that they were not aware of. They were the messengers after all. However, she began to read the messages of brother Branham that they did not have access to in Iran and soon realized that, indeed, the rapture lays inside the messages. Sister Maryam said, "Every time that I read a book and listened to a sermon, I specifically thanked God both for the translator of these messages, and for myself for being in such a place that I can understand these kinds of things. I pray that God will bring this reality to those who are not able to listen or understand." Now her desire is to understand and listen to all of brother Branham's messages, as well as to read them in their original language.

CHAPTER 7

ESTABLISHING THE DOCTRINE

In 2015, we really focused on and emphasized: adoption and election from eternity to eternity. During the second quarter, we went into the churches and preached on holiness to the Lord. It was a time of hitting some things hard, and we could see that some people were uncomfortable and some did not like it. It was difficult to recognize any fruits of our labor during this time.

Upon our return to Eskisehir, however, to God's glory, we noted people were living in obedience to the word of God and the Message. Anytime I present holiness, I always try to bring out that the commandments come not to make us feel a heavy burden, but they come for our joy. And we could see that the Message had become a joy to many of the people. One of the sisters testified, when she came to Turkey she was very depressed. But once she got to know the true reality of what the Message is, she said, "It is not a burden to obey but it is literally joy." She listens to the translations on her phone while she is working around the house and is consistently feeding on the Message.

We had another ministers' meeting in July of 2015. Brother Dale Smith, Evangelist from Beaufort, South Carolina joined us and we had wonderful meetings. We delved into the *Church Order* message and taught the people how the prophet structured: conducting services. We also went into the coming of the Lord and went more in depth into Godhead. Finally, I went through *The Seven Seals* as this group of believers had never been taught about them.

During this time, we were planting the teachings of the message in the hearts of the ministers and believers working with us. It was a time of laboring in the Word and doctrine. At some points, we felt discouraged because you couldn't visibly see tremendous results, as you would when doing evangelism, or having prayer for the sick. But it was this time that deeply established many of the ministers in the Word, so that true fruit of the reality of this message could come forth. One of the ministers we worked with for a short time in Eskisehir told us his testimony and we wanted to share it with you.

Brother Arshad

Brother Arshad is a pastor in Turkey. He is a former Muslim from Rasht,

Iran who gave his heart to Christ and became a

minister in Iran despite much persecution.

Islam is a way of life in Iran, and he was born and raised in a very religious and strict Muslim family. His mother often attended courses on the Quran and desired that her children would follow in her footsteps. As a result, she was very strict with them. Arshad grew up participating in the prayers, attending religious ceremonies, and was brought up Islamic throughout his school years. When Arshad eventually converted to Christianity, his mother cast him, his wife, and his son out of her house, refusing for a whole year to have any type of contact or relationship with them.

Arshad first heard the gospel in 2001. One scripture stood out to him: "You shall know the truth and the truth shall set you free." He constantly thought on this verse but was unable to understand it's meaning. He contacted a pastor in the Church of Iran and after talking with him, he received Jesus as his Lord and savior.

There were a few others who also accepted Christianity, and the four of them began to meet in a small basement to hear the scriptures. God was with them and grew their numbers from the 325 people they were led to reach out to. Five years later, in 2006, the first bout of persecution from the VEVAK (Iran's version of our CIA, FBI and NSA) began in their church and Arshad was arrested. The church continued their services despite this difficult situation and Arshad was released a few months later. He was not yet a minister but, from that time on, he felt the call to be a pastor to serve the Lord; however, he still questioned himself, "Do you think that you can serve the Lord?" He spent much time in prayer until he received a promise from the Lord that one day he would serve him. So, he kept praying and worshipping God and asking for his leading in the ministry. He felt the Lord wanted to use him in the city of Karaj, Turkey and he and a few other brothers began to minister.

Pressure from the VEVAK kept increasing to the point where they were unable to have fellowship together in one place. They had to scatter and they circulated their fellowshipping throughout the city. Arshad and 3 other brothers were summoned by the VEVAK. They were interrogated and asked to sign a paper promising not to do any further ministering. But the brothers had just been looking to increase their services because of the increase in believers and they refused to sign the paper.

In 2013, the VEVAK invaded Arshad's house, twice. The first time he was not home but they confiscated many of his personal belongings including his cell phone, laptops, books, and his Bible. Two months later, he and the other brothers were summoned again where they were once again threatened and told to make a deal and sign a paper to end their proselytizing. Again, the brothers refused.

One morning, at 9:30am, the VEVAK searched Arshad's house for a second time and then arrested him. It was much harder this time. For 85 days, they interrogated him and then took him to court and then brought him back and interrogated him some more. They transferred him to a central prison where he stayed for two months before they put him on trial. He was sentenced to serve six years in prison and was exiled to south Iran. He did some research of the prison they were sending him to and found it was a very violent prison, for the worst of the worst criminals. He remembers thinking, "How do I find a way out of this situation?" But no solution came. He kept praying, "God, how is this possible? How are you going to let me step inside this prison?" He was met with silence from the Lord, but he still believed the Lord was listening because that is his promise. After some time of struggling within himself, he reached a point where he completely surrendered to God.

Following that surrender, a door opened to appeal the sentence. The attorney hired for him, told him not to get his hopes up; but they appealed anyway and were summoned to court. They had a kind judge and Arshad convinced himself that the best-case scenario would be to have his exile removed and two years of his sentence removed.

The night before they appeared in court, Arshad was again struggling with surrender. As he laid in bed he told the Lord, "Oh my Lord, you are the one . . . If you want me to be devoted, I surrender all my ideas to you." A peace that he had not experienced for a long time under those trying circumstances washed over him. Five days later they called his name, which was unusual because there were many prisoners with longer sentences. He went before the officer and the officer said, "You are being released."

Arshad said, "How is that possible? It is not possible, it is impossible!"

The officer responded, "Do not argue with me. This is your release paper," and he offered him the document.

As Arshad walked down the hall he thought, "Maybe they are going to exile me and this is a lie. God, where are they taking me?" They put him in a dark room with one other man. He asked the man why he was there and the man said he had just been arrested. Arshad thought, "If I am to be released, why did they put me in the same cell with him?" Memories of past situations clouded his mind until that still small voice reminded him, "You committed everything into my hands." The Lord's reminder encouraged and cheered his heart and all worry was allayed.

Approximately 30 minutes later, they called him again to fill out some final paperwork and then he stepped out of prison. He looked up at the sky and said, "It is impossible, Lord God. I had six years!" At that same moment, he remembered how God had miraculously opened the prison cell for Peter and it was as if history had just repeated itself, for him. Arshad was so grateful to the Lord and realized that when he was completely surrendered to the Lord, God was able to do everything and glorify his own name.

Arshad testifies that even though this was a very difficult time, he learned much from the Lord. He met

God face to face, metaphorically, and praises the Lord for being counted worthy to be among those to be persecuted for his name.

Brother Keyvan

Brother Keyvan Rajabi is an Evangelist and Pastor from Rasht, Iran. He was confronted with the Christian faith in 2002 by a man that he worked with. The man had a New Testament hidden in his desk and as they were working together Keyvan happened to see it. So, he asked the man about it. The man was surprised that Keyvan was interested and so he began to share the Gospel with him. In fact, the man worked the morning shift and Keyvan worked the afternoon shift so they would not normally be together, but the man was asked to stay on his shift an extra hour and as a result met Keyvan. When he heard the message for the first time he had such a good feeling about it. During this time, he had another friend that was an atheist and was causing him to start to question the Muslim faith.

Keyvan struggling in his mind for several months about what he heard. After first hearing the gospel Keyvan says that he kept hearing the voice of the accuser of the brethren, "Keyvan, what are you doing? It's wrong to leave Islam and convert to Christianity." Then fear gripped him, but after reading a little booklet called *The Footprints of God in the Plan of Salvation* everything became clear in his mind and by God's grace His heart was opened to the truth. From the very beginning, he had a burning desire to share the glorious message he had received with everyone he could.

As Keyvan was growing in his understanding the message of the hour began to completely transform his life. God began to deal with him to deliver him from the spirit of Islamic fanaticism. After that the Lord began to deal with his attitude towards people, his temper was gone, before when things went wrong he would lash out in anger and begin to break things in his house. In the past if someone would wrong him he wouldn't stop thinking about how he could get back at them, but after coming to Christ he realized that he didn't think that way anymore.

Keyvan still has the same desire today, to bring this message to the lost and dying. He desires to continue in this same ministry wherever God sends him. Keyvan says that the greatest things that have ever happened to him are coming to Christ and ministering Christ to others.

He received the end time message through the very same person that shared the Gospel with him. After going through the plan of salvation he introduced the message to him. When Keyvan first heard about the message of the hour it was a tremendous joy that he experienced.

After his conversion, the great joy that he had was pushing him forward. And since Keyvan was experiencing transformation in his own life, he started reaching out to his family. He started to talk about the love of God to his wife. And after that he started to speak to his mother who was a serious Muslim. And every chance that he had with his relatives, he was witnessing about Christ and sharing the joy that he received through Jesus Christ with other people.

Through the studying of the bible, he was helping other Muslims, who were living a lie, to understand they were going the wrong way. He had such a joy and peace and his life was so drastically changed that his wife came to Christ. Even his mother left Islam to turn to Christ which it was a miracle. Keyvan's mother was even willing to attend the local church which could be a great danger to her. It was after three or four months of being a Christian that he started to lead souls to Christ.

Keyvan shared the Gospel with at least a thousand people in Iran. He has witnessed the work of God in his country through the anointed ministry that he had. It was an incredible testimony to him to see every soul who would bow before the Word and receive it.

Time after time he would face questions that he'd never heard before, but the Holy Spirit would lead him to scripture where he could answer them. Not only was the person convinced, but Keyvan knew that it was not him. The person would come to Christ and it would increase his faith and encourage him, and much of the strength that he has in his own Christian walk he attributes to the testimonies that he witnessed in his own ministry.

Around 2005 or 2006, the government of Iran

started persecuting the church. VEVAK arrested ministers and asked those who had been coming to the church for a while to report in for questioning. Their questions were related to how did you come to Christ? Who shared the gospel with you? Who is coming to the services? How many people are coming together?

And it was just a drop of the rain of prosecution that was coming for them. On another day, they summoned his mom for questioning and frightened her. Since Keyvan was her only child, they told her that they would kill him; it stressed her out so much that it came to the point that when his mom was leaving the office and coming down the stairs, she felt so disoriented that she couldn't even find her way back home. And she said that, "After two or three minutes I was walking purposeless down the street, I realized where I am and what I should do".

But it's interesting that when the interrogator started questioning Keyvan, he felt an anointing from heaven on his body. When he first entered VEVAK's office he was scared, but when the questions started he had such a strength and power that he started witnessing to that interrogator. And the person told Keyvan, 'Hey, wait a minute. Are you sharing the gospel with me?' 'God wants you to be saved as well. I'm pretty sure that one day God will get a hold of you', Keyvan replied. And with mocking and scoffing at him, 'I hope that it happens one day', he said. And I said, 'Amen.'

And ever since then he's been waiting to see the fulfillment of that prayer. Because years after that, he saw that interrogator again. But first time it was interesting that they met face to face, but years after that he was standing behind him. He couldn't see him but he could recognize that this is the same person from his voice. Keyvan even told him that, 'I recognized you; you're the same person.' And the interrogator said, 'Okay.' Keyvan then asked him, "Has God gotten a hold of you yet, after all these years?" He refused to answer but Keyvan was sure that the Word had an impact on him. Maybe he couldn't make a confession because he feared losing his job title or income, but the way he treated Keyvan, he could see that the Word had an impact.

The biggest persecution that brother Keyvan faced in his ministry was what he went through in 2010; because he oversaw holding the Christmas banquet that year. He oversaw ministering the Word and he had a message from the Lord. And VEVAK tried to interrupt the service and prevent them from having the service in the auditorium in Rasht. But by God's grace they had the service because they had no fear. And it made VEVAK upset because they didn't want them to have the service but they did it anyway because they had the leading from the Lord that there are souls that ought to hear this message today.

He also recalls while he was at the pulpit, telling the congregation that there I have no fear today. But God taught him a lesson even in his statement. A week or ten days after the Christmas service, security agents raided our home. He was ministering the Word in a service in another area and they confiscated everything related to Christianity in his home. They took his computer and everything that was related to his faith and they were waiting for him to arrive home so they could take him into custody.

The first week he had the same strength but after that, during the second week, because there was no progress in his case and he didn't know what was going on, suddenly, he felt fear grip me. And they made threats to his life and tortured him mentally and physically. This was around the same time that Brother Youcef Nadarkhani was on death row. And for seventeen or eighteen days, he was not allowed to contact his family.

On one hand, he knew his family was confused and afraid and on the other hand he was scared, thinking, "what if they hang me?" And eventually God reminded him of Saint Peter and he heard a voice telling him, 'Do you remember a week ago you said that you had no fear? And I could see that you were being proud and I allowed you to be brought here so you can experience the fear'.

Because of that he started praying, 'Lord God I learned my lesson and if you let me walk out of this prison I promise that I will go forward with more wisdom in my ministry and I will not be proud of myself anymore'. And so, he had to surrender myself to some things that the interrogator asked him about.

One of the terms was to stop talking to any other Shiite Muslim regarding the Christian faith. The second one was to avoid starting any home churches anymore, and do not go to any church services personally. But it was interesting that they didn't have anything regarding his faith. He realized that this was something that God did not allow them to attack by trying to get him to recant. He believes it was because of the fear that he was facing and if they would have asked him to renounce his faith he might have done that. Everything that he was facing was a lesson that God was teaching him.

After twenty-one days in custody, he was released. Unfortunately, this fear caused him to isolate himself and he quit his ministry for about a year. But after that time God started working with him again. And then he started following up with the church members that he used to work with. Previously, in the family visits, he used to go and visit people and start talking about the Christian faith and ministering the Word.

And all along, he used to receive calls from VEVAK agents and they were watching him. They knew every little detail about his life to the point that the same agent who interrogated him called him and said, "Are you sharing the gospel with people again?" I told them, "I haven't formed any home church or anything, but you should know that normally when two Christians come together, all they talk about is the Word of God. Just like when two thieves come together they start planning on a robbery. Or when two Muslims come together on the roof they talk about Islam. And it's pretty normal when it's believer or a Christian that I will answer the questions regarding their Christian faith and we have fellowship."

The terms were not that he couldn't speak with people and not having a church service. They never told him that he couldn't be in contact with any Christians. For example, he used to talk about Christian faith with his wife and mother, and there is nothing in the terms about that. Then he started to end his isolation and getting back on track again.

Whenever believers would come together he asked them not to bring their cellphones. He also asked them not to speak about church or fellowship times over the phone with one another. He would also change the day, time and location of church services every week; to the point that, by God's grace, he was able to baptize many people inside Iran.

In 2014, God provided and opened the door so that he could make a trip to Turkey. He went to a minister's meeting as an encouragement in his faith. When he returned to Iran he faced another wave of persecution. They summoned him to VEVAK's facility again. They were asking for explanations about "why did go to Turkey? What will you do now that you came back? Do you want to start a church again? If you are doing that we will exile you to worst parts of the country; Sistan or Baluchestan or Zahedan." These questions showed that they were fishing for information. And since he had the experience of being interrogated in 2005 and 2006, he tried to just go to general answers, not in detail. Or he talked about people that they already knew were Christians.

But he didn't share any details about new converts. They didn't even know that he had baptized people recently. And he was afraid they had access to this information and that they would cause trouble for him.

And it was around the same time they started arresting other ministers. But since they were not aware of his activities, he started praying and asking God for wisdom. He said in prayer, "Lord I cannot go through these kinds of things anymore, please send me to a place so I have more freedom to do my ministry and I don't have to face these kinds of dangers." In 2010 when some people left the country, they suggested that he leave also. But he didn't leave since he didn't have any leading from the Lord and he told the believers who were leaving that he must stay because God is not done with him in this country.

Because after he was released in 2010, he was not doing any kind of ministry, but after eighteen months, he resumed to his ministry and started sharing the gospel. He started spreading the message amongst believers and because of his ministry, a thousand people came to Christ.

During the persecution in 2014, he felt peace from the Lord to leave the country. As God moved Abraham from his former land, God told him that this is the time for him to leave your country. He felt led to leave so he could share the message with more souls beyond the borders in Iran; because there are souls that need to hear the message of the hour but he didn't know which city he should go to. So, he left and went to Turkey.

Keyvan was praying about this and thinking about which city he should settle in. He felt that God didn't want him to go to Eskisehir or Denizli. Before praying about it he thought that it should be one of those cities but God had a different plan and sent him to a city he had never heard of before; Burdur. But he's living in Isparta now because when he went to UNHCR to register, the interpreter in that office recommended that he to go to Burdur because it was close to Denizli. But God wanted him thirty minutes away from Burdur in the city of Isparta. And in fact, the place that they are having the services in now is a gift from the Lord.

For a week, he was looking for a place to rent for the church but couldn't find any. On the seventh day, he knelt before the Lord and prayed, "Father, you sent me here to minister, so please provide me with a place." He didn't know any Turkish, so he went to a real estate office with a friend that was living there already, who could speak some Turkish. The real estate person brought him to the same place they're renting now. It has a very big living room and is the perfect place to turn into a church.

Interestingly, the devil wanted to strike at them through the downstairs neighbors that complained about them to the police office. The police came to the front door but never came up to the church apartment because there was a fish market downstairs and the owner was a friend of Keyvan's, and he stopped the police from going upstairs. And after defending us in front of the police, that guy came upstairs and talked to Keyvan and said "the neighbors are complaining about noise. Your downstairs neighbor has complained about you." But something was telling Keyvan "since God provided this place, he's more than able to protect it as well."

He's not supposed to be there but he is living there now, the police tried to come to the front door, but they couldn't come up to us because God wants them there because he has souls that need to hear the gospel and the end time message. And Keyvan is confident the Lord will protect him.

Keyvan's desire and purpose in life is to be able to minister the Lord to people, sharing the Word with every soul no matter where he goes. When he first came to Turkey he was planning to go to another country through the refugee process, but the day that he knelt and prayed before the Lord and he provided a place, the thinking that he had to go to another country went away and he began to settle down and not worry about that anymore. Keyvan said, "I told the Lord that wherever you send me I know you will provide me with everything and I will be able to minister to you with joy whether in Turkey or any other country."

When he was sharing the Gospel with some individuals he could see that they were coming to just to question and argue with the Gospel. For example, someone would hear about the Christian faith through a friend then he would get in contact with the me; but after hearing the Gospel, he would stop in the middle of the conversation. From that point Keyvan was leading the conversation and at the end of the conversation the person would say, 'I want to receive Christ' it was amazing.

Keyvan shared an amazing testimony with me. There was a man deep in religious faith in Islam. Keyvan had three meetings with the man already and he was on his way for a fourth and he was praying that if he'll accept the Gospel today that's fine, otherwise he's done and won't go back to him anymore. In that meeting, once again, he was jumping from one question to another and he was trying to challenge the Christian faith in front of his friends. Keyvan heard a voice in his mind that said, "Stop talking. Close your bible. Go lay your hands on him and start praying."

When Keyvan laid hands on him and started praying and the Lord revealed the spirit of religiousness, this person was crying and shedding tears. Keyvan went back and sat down. And then that person came to him, hugged him and started crying again. Keyvan was surprised thinking; "what's going on?" And so, he asked the man, 'What's the reason for this?' He said, "When you were praying for me, eventually a curtain was removed from in front of me and everything you were telling me about Christianity and Islam became a reality to me." He kept telling Keyvan that a curtain was removed. Keyvan was happy because he knew that God's Spirit was moving in that man's life.

Working with Brother Keyvan in Turkey

Brother Keyvan is a now minister in a message church in Isparta, Turkey. When we first met Keyvan, he had a lot of pride in his spiritual walk, due to his accomplishments in the Lord. While there was a great sincerity in what he believed, due to the message background he was a part of, there was a lack in understanding regarding the true nature of the message. It was necessary to be very up front with him and explain this very clearly. We explained, he may know about five percent, but he insisted that he knew the Message very well. I asked him how many sermons were translated and he said forty-five. I asked if he would explain for me *Christ is the Mystery of God Revealed* and what the three-fold purpose is. He said that that Message was not translated. I then asked if he had read the *An Exposition of the Seven Church Ages book*. He again said it was not translated. I asked if I should continue. I was determined to bring the point home that every one of us needs to learn and grow. There is more of the Message to grasp and more to further be revealed to us. We need to continually allow for correction on smaller points within the understanding that we already have. He listened, even though he also expressed his displeasure of my assessment.

He attended the ministers' meetings and began to see the many details the Message covers about so many scriptural things. The night before our last day of services, Keyvan came and asked us to pray for him. He said that he had a spirit on him that made him want to research everything to its fullest degree before he could accept it. But after listening to the last few services he said he realized that it is good to research and to study, but at some point, he had to submit and surrender to the fact that there is a vindicated prophet. He recognized that God had vindicated the prophet in such a way that he could put confidence in what he said. As we prayed, Keyvan began weeping.

The next day as brother Dale Smith and I preached, Keyvan could not stop crying. He had reached that place of surrender where the revelation came through, into his heart. He became a completely different man than the one we first met.

He began preaching the Message in the local church and the entire church left except for three people. There was another group of about fifty people that the denominational church had been mistreating and had refused to baptize. Kavon began meeting with these people one by one and he found them to be sincere people that had truly given their hearts to the Lord. He invited them to church and began teaching them. He also took them on a day trip to the Mediterranean Sea on the southern coast of Turkey where he baptized thirty-eight of them. There are about fifteen more that still need to be baptized. Every Wednesday, week by week, he reads through a sermon and comments on it to make sure the people are understanding it. He wants them to know and understand the Message and that they are following the word of the prophet God sent. The Lord is blessing his ministry and we are so thankful for him. Another brother that we started working with around the same time was a close friend of brother Nehemiah in Tehran, whom he led to the Lord.

CHAPTER 8

GETTING DEEPLY ROOTED

Brother Omid

Brother Omid Kaleybar Nejad was born in Tehran, Iran in 1985 where he was raised Muslim with his brother and two sisters. In 2006, as a college student in Computer Software Engineering, he had become disgusted with his experiences with the different facets of Islam as presented by the Iranian government and her religious leaders. He became more interested in finding the answers to his questions on Islam and read as many books as he could to try to resolve his issues and oppositions to what he was constantly preached.

Meanwhile, he was hired to teach a course on computer programming in Roshangar Institute in Tehran. It was here that he met and hit it off with one of his students, brother Nehemiah Ardavan, who was six years older than himself. Brother Nehemiah had converted to Christianity only a few months earlier, and the two of them had many exciting and life changing conversations about Christianity.

Eventually brother Nehemiah introduced brother Omid to his home church pastor, brother Jamshid, and brother Omid began reading some books on Christianity. The more he read, the more he saw the validity of the Bible and Jesus, and his feelings grew stronger about the reality of who Jesus is. He had mixed feelings. As a Muslim, he had come to realize that Islam could not resolve his questions, while he was feeling very comfortable with the concepts of Christianity and the teachings of Jesus. But if he were to convert to Christianity, he could not face his family, friends, and the overzealous government policies. Yet staying with Islam would mean forfeiting the happiness and peace he was beginning to feel within himself.

Brother Omid prayed to the Lord, asking Him to show him the right way. He received his answer after an inner awakening experience and spiritual encounter with Jesus, and he accepted Jesus as his own personal Savior.

He began to attend the home church held in brother Nehemiah's home. This small group chose not to attend the official Armenian Apostolic in Tehran because they were concerned they would be arrested by government agents. According to the Islamic Republic of Iran, renouncing Islam is a capital offense. In some cases it is labeled as a blasphemy and insult to the religion, which could potentially be used to prosecute them for apostasy. Therefore, they met in a home and grew to 15 people.

Brother Omid was continually blessed as he learned more about his new faith through the weekly meetings, and he became committed to spreading the teachings of Jesus and the Gospel to anyone he could. He designed a professional website called **PersianMission.com** under the guidance of his pastor. Behrouz Sadegh-Khanjani. The website included sections of the Bible to download, weekly sermons, and some evangelical books. By the grace of Lord, the strong internet presence helped the church to attract more attendees and support across Iran and beyond. He also designed and created CDs of his pastor's weekly sermons and shipped and distributed them to the public.

With the increased publicity, the home church grew in number and the Iranian secret service became alarmed. At least once a month they called in the pastor for questioning and interrogation about the church's activities. Finally, on June 18, 2010, they arrested brother Omid and 5 others during their weekly prayer meeting. Brother Omid was handcuffed and brought to his home where they confiscated his computers, external hard drives, books and CD's. They imprisoned him in Evin prison in Tehran for 19 days, including 10 days in solitary confinement. He endured constant and long interrogations. They kept threatening to hang him since he converted from Islam to Christianity and for publicizing his faith through the persianmission.com website. They also accused him of having relationships with American and Israeli organizations to plot against the Islamic Republic of Iran.

His parents were finally able to bail him from the prison using the deed to their house as a guarantee. He was let go on bail with the condition that he would not go back to the church and to sever all relationships with his Christian friends. He also was not officially free, as he had to wait for the final decision regarding his case by the Islamic court in Tehran. However, regardless of the secret polices threats, upon being released from Evin prison, he resumed attending his church meetings secretly. Brother Omid was still serving his mandatory military service during this time and it was not long before the military intelligence service arrested him and began interrogating him again in Havanirooz Prison.

In September of 2011, he finally received his dreaded court judgement and sentence. He was officially placed on probation for five years which meant he could no longer have any contact or participation in any Christian activities. He was under a great deal of mental pressure. Any violations against his probation would have meant that his family would lose the deed to their house that they had put up for his bail, and he would go back to Evin prison, enduring continuous torturing by the secret agents.

Due to these conditions, he decided to lay low for a while. However, his conscious would not allow him to be quiet so he created a weblog and began writing about his horrendous experience and the fate of his fellow Christians in Evin prison. It was not long until the government also blocked this site as well.

Every two to three months he was summoned to the government secret and intelligence service in Tehran.

He was constantly threatened to stay away from the Christian faith or face the consequence of being hanged. The pressure mounted as he remained under constant watch and interrogations, and despite his so-called freedom, he found himself living in his own sort of prison. On May 18, 2014, he decided to free himself and left Iran to seek refuge in Turkey.

It was very difficult to leave his country and family for good. He had been making a good living as the IT Director for several hospitals in Tehran, he was married, and he was prosperous - except, he still had a big empty hole in his heart. Upon his arrival in Turkey, he was transferred to Sivas, a small town in the center of Turkey. It was there he finally felt free and able to practice his faith and devotion to the Lord Jesus.

2 weeks later he had designed a Christian website, churchiran.com, where he reported the status of Iranian Christians who were arrested and persecuted in Iran. He was positive that educating and making the public aware of the lack of religious freedom and tremendous pressure of the government toward religious minorities would help his fellow Christians. He strongly believed that the ongoing interviews and reports of the struggles of fellow Christians by the Voice of America had had an influence on his release as well. However, Iran intelligence discovered that brother Omid held the domain and website for churchiran.com and yet again blocked his site.

Brother Omid experienced many ups and downs during this time but the Lord supported him in them all.

He believed that this move would increase his faith. Finally, after 3 years without fellowship, he attended his first Sunday service at brother Nehemiah's home. Brother Omid also now had access to the many messages that brother Nehemiah had translated into Farsi, and he had a special interest and desire to read these messages since the limited access and pressures in Iran had not allowed for it before. Now after two and a half years, he can see the positive impact and influence the message of the hour has had on his life.

Today he serves as an associate minister in Sivas as well as handling the websites <u>peygham.net</u> and <u>PTMradio.com</u>. This work has continued to improve his faith and to help him understand more fully God's map in the end times by His vindicated prophet, William Branham.

Continuing the History of the Work in Turkey

While on the third quarter trip in 2015, Nehemiah and I had some outstanding testimonies that took place from the prayer lines we held in each of the churches. In Isparta, Turkey there was someone that had been suffering for quite some time from severe, daily migraines. They came through the prayer line and testified the following week that they no longer suffered from migraines since that service.

During the fourth quarter trip of the same year, I spoke about The Sovereignty of God in Election. I could see that many were not grasping pre-destination very well, due to the misconceptions they brought from their denominational Message church. As we began to go through the doctrine, you could see a rest and peace settle into the people.

We also had the opportunity to meet Brother Behnam Irani's family and fellowship with them. They had recently fled Iran and were going through the refugee process in Turkey. They felt very much alone, so we took a day off to take them to see Laodicea, so they could have a chance to rest and have some fun. It was a blessing to see them leave their troubles behind for a day to take pictures, relax and enjoy themselves.

In 2016, we made three trips to Turkey. In March 2016 we visited Sivas, Eskisehir, Isparta and Denizli. We held three services in each city, except for Sivas, where we had two; we covered "Seven Thunders of Revelation 10", the "Seventh Seal", "We Are Not of This World", "Obedience is Better than Sacrifice", "Thirsting for Life.' Brother Nehemiah and Brother Dale Smith travelled with me during that time. The most notable testimony from this trip was when I was in Isparta, preaching on "Obedience is Better than Sacrifice" and as the service started I prayed that "the Holy Spirit would fall upon the people while the Word was being preached" and one of the sisters in the church testified that when I prayed that a fire came down upon her body and for the next day she was walking around the house singing and shouting to the Lord.

In our July 2016 missions trip, I traveled with Nehemiah once again. We visited two churches this time, taking a different approach, working more deeply in each of these cities, Isparta and Eskisehir. Our purpose was to spend more time there delivering more teaching there. We also had our third annual Persian ministers meeting where we opened it up to some new believers who were on fire for God to do something for him. We covered Godhead, Church Order and the Grace of God delivered to us through the message of the hour. Two of the newer believers attending testified that they were born again during these services. Shahin and Keyvan also took two services for the first time during our minister's meetings and did an amazing job, it literally brought tears to my eyes to hear them bringing forth the true revelation of this Word in this day. As we continued to Eskisehir we ministered to the believers and baptized five new believers.

On our fourth quarter trip, we visited Denizli, Isparta and Kayseri. Petros, Nehemiah and I were together in Denizli and each of us ministered there. Then we split up and Nehemiah and I went to Isparta and had a few services and then went on to Kayseri to work with a group of new believers as we seek to plant a new church there.

In April 2017, I met up with brother Omid and he translated for me. We held one service in Kayseri with brand new believers. Then we went on to Denizli and worked with the local church there. I spoke on the subject "Chosen by God" and "Tithes and Offerings". While in Denizli a sister from Kayseri called, her mother was in the hospital and seemingly had a stroke. The mother was unresponsive so I told the sister to place her hands on her mother and to believe and we would pray. In 15 minutes, we received a phone call that her mother was completely healed, was sitting in the chair and talking to people. Blessed be the name of the Lord.

Then we went on to Isparta where we held our first Bible Mysteries Conference. During this conference, a woman from a Baptist service came to attend. She walked into the service and saw our outreach materials, one of them having a picture of brother Branham on it. She said, "where is he?" Brother Keyvan responded that he had died quite some time ago. She said, "no, I just saw him a moment ago, he looked younger and had more hair, but he greeted me as I came into the building." When she was informed that he was dead for a long time she was shocked and so was her family. They were eager to learn more about his ministry and doctrine and took home with them all the materials we had there and are now learning and growing in the message of the hour.

Our Ministry Vision

There is a two-fold plan for the work in Turkey. We

are a team of ministers working for one purpose. First, we want to bring the gospel to Muslims in such a way that we do not ignore the Message but also do not project the style of Billy Graham. Instead, we start right away with serpent seed doctrine. When Muslims can understand serpent seed, they can grasp why Messiah, a man, had to die on a cross for their sins. Otherwise, their concept of the Message may be corrupt. When we are home we spend most of our time on Skype with brethren: one week, we have private interviews with each of the ministers, and the next, we have a Bible study with different groups of ministers. The second part of our plan is to begin to introduce the end time message to them. We start to show them Scriptural water baptism, then to the Godhead and why the Trinity of three persons is not the true biblical teaching. After that we discuss why women preachers are wrong, then we begin to show them the truth about the seven church ages in Revelation 2 and 3 and that each age has messengers. Then we go to the opening of the word in the end time that is told about in Daniel 12, then tie that into Revelation 5, 6 and 10. After that we cover Malachi 4:5-6 and Luke 17:30. Then we show how these Scriptures were fulfilled in the message of brother Branham.

CONCLUSION

As you have read these testimonies and the history of the missions work that we are doing you might be amazed and challenged in your faith by the stories of these believers. I hope you can see the reality that God directs our lives, and that even through many difficulties it is His sovereign grace that sustains each of us. Our vision and mission remains the same; minister to Iranian's by bringing them the Gospel and teaching them the message. There is certainly much more to do.

I have worked closely with Iranian's now since 2009 and it is filled with many ups and downs. I'm always amazed to hear their stories, how they lived and their faith thrived through such great pressure and difficulties. I know each and every one of these believers. I have seen them go through many trials and difficulties. I love them with all my heart and am so thankful for each of them. My desire grows each day to be a courageous Christian that not only makes it through, but thrives in the midst of great trials and difficulties and that doesn't blink at the dangers. Christ lived and died for me, now it is my life to live and die, if he so chooses, for him. The problem sometimes is that we wait until the moment of truth to decide if we are willing to die. When we come to Christ we should make that decision immediately. Jesus tells us that to be His disciple we must be willing to take up our cross and follow Him. That means we are dead men walking! Our decision is made, we choose death before denying Christ or moving away from His perfect will.

To follow the latest updates about the missions work and to support this ministry go to: presenttruthmn.com

BIBLIOGRAPHY

1. All Bible verses referenced are taken from the KJV
2. Quotes from William Marrion Branham are taken from Voice of God Recordings table.branham.org

Made in the USA
Columbia, SC
12 April 2024

34149238R00088